SAVINI DIAMOND

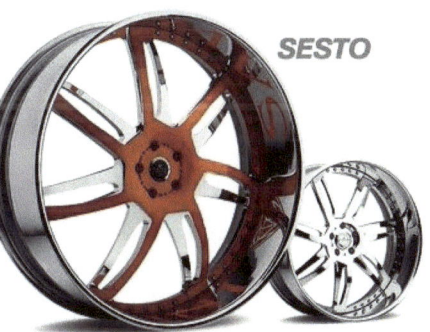
SESTO

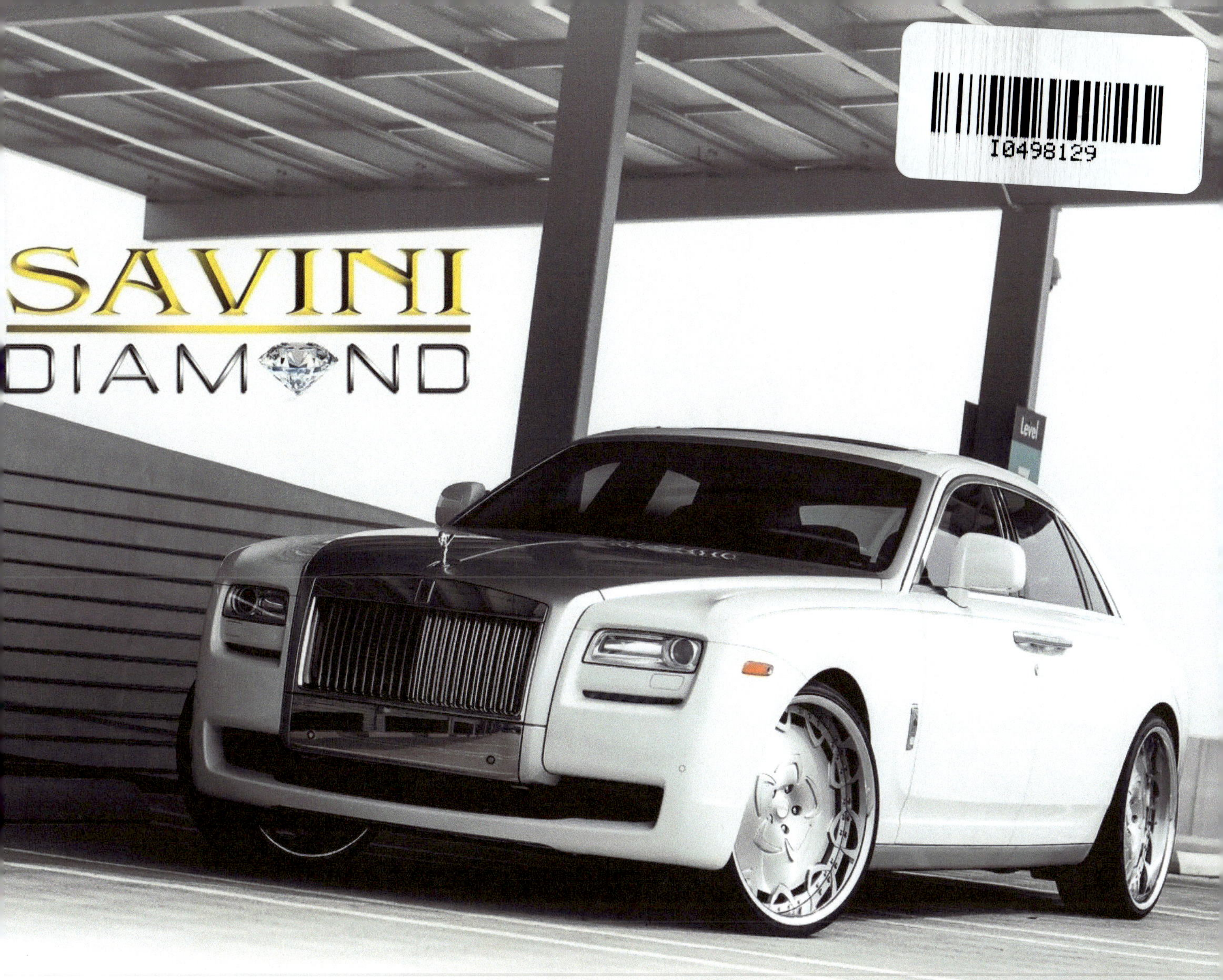

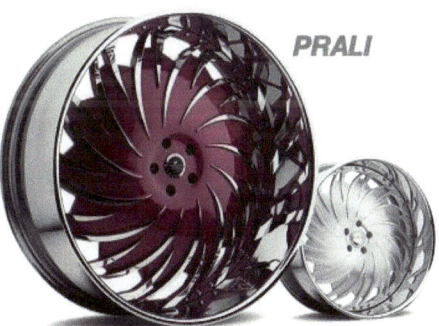
PRALI

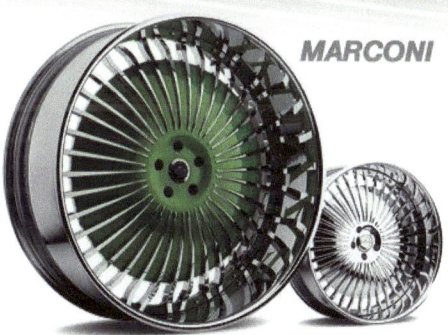
MARCONI

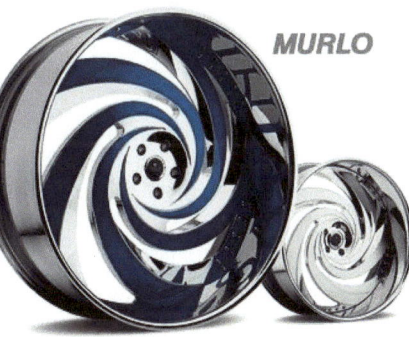
MURLO

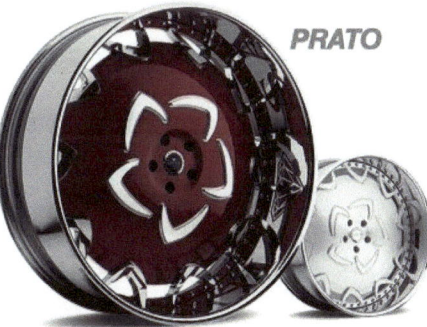
PRATO

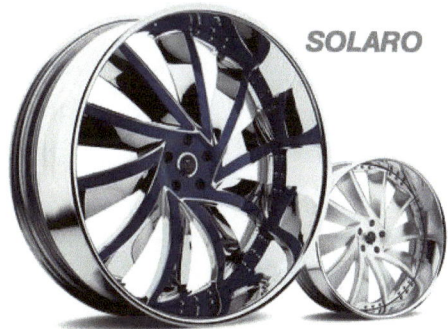
SOLARO

SAVINIWHEELS.COM | 866.779.4646

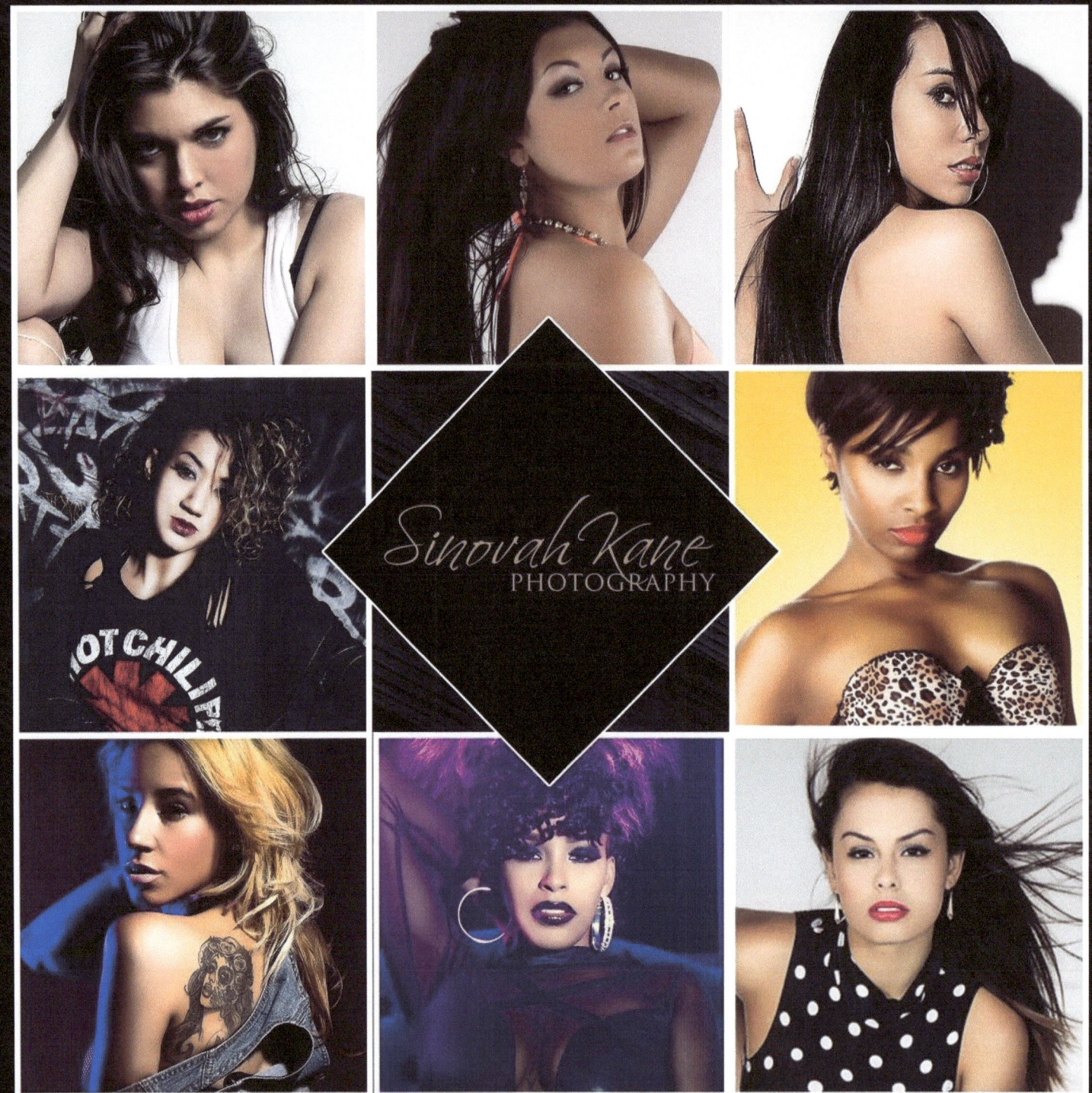

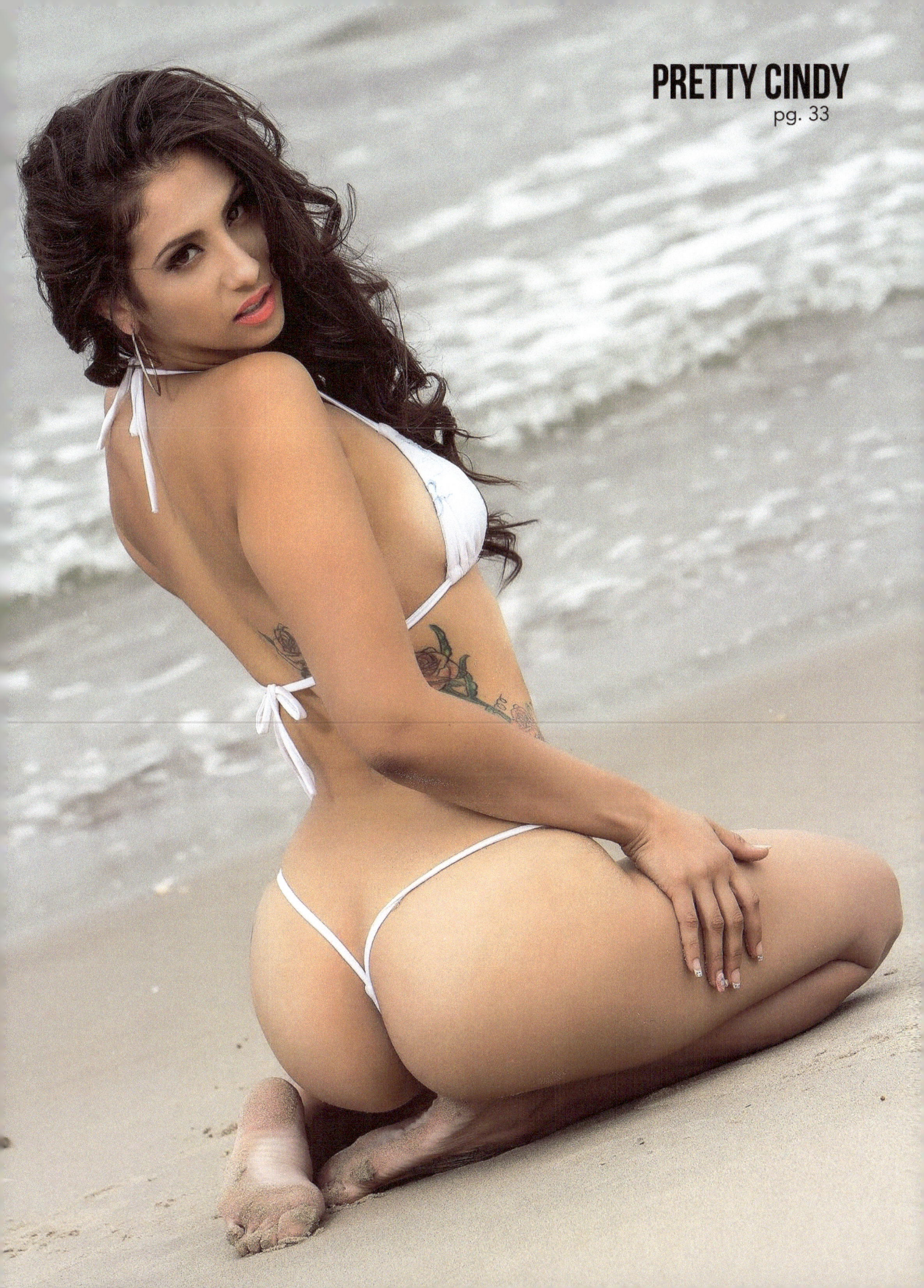

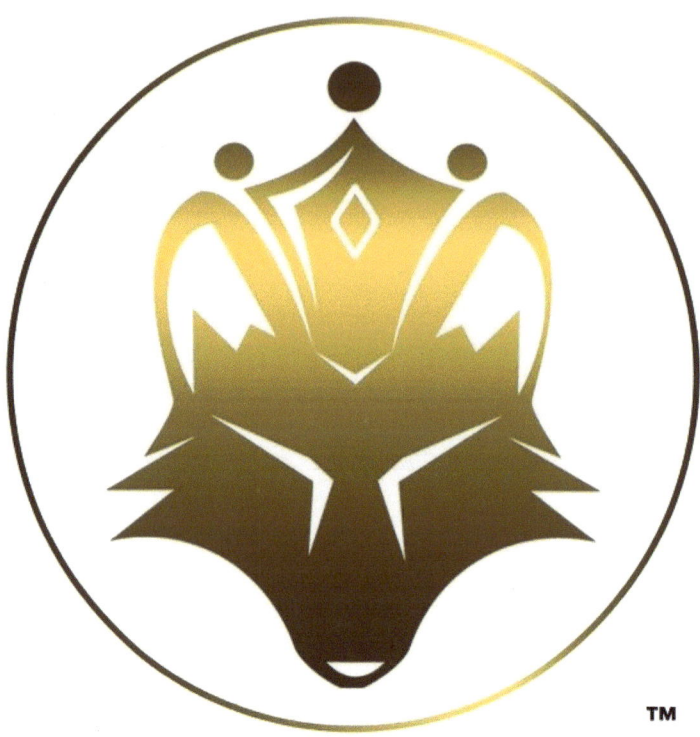

WWW.FOXTAILMAG.COM

FOXTAIL Magazine (ISSN #978-1981-678334), Issue #1 (January 2015), is published bi-monthly by **Foxtail, Inc.**, 945 W. Agatite Ave., Chicago, IL 60640. The subscription rate is $24.95 per year. One-year subscriptions rates: U.S., $24.95; Canada, $54.95; for all other countries, $84.95 in prepaid U.S. funds. Periodicals postage paid at Chicago, IL and additional mailing offices. POSTMASTER: Send address changes to *FOXTAIL Magazine*, 945 W. Agatite Ave., Chicago, IL 60640,. Reproduction or use of any part of Issue #1 (January 2015) of *FOXTAIL Magazine* without the written consent of the publisher is prohibited. Return postage must accompany all manuscripts, drawings or photographs. All manuscripts, drawings or photographs sent to *FOXTAIL Magazine* will be treated as unconditionally assigned for publication and copyright purposes and are subject to the magazine's right to edit and comment editorially. *FOXTAIL Magazine* assumes no responsibility for the advertisements made herein or the quality and availability of the products advertised herein. *FOXTAIL Magazine* assumes no responsibility to determine whether the people whose photographs or statements appear in such advertisements have, in fact, endorsed such products or consented to the use of their names or photographs, or the statements attributed to them. The publisher is exempt from the record-keeping requirements and disclosure statements mandated by 18 U.S. Code, Section 2257 A - C and the pertinent regulations, 28 C.F.R. Ch.1, Part 75, since all of such material falls within the exempted material set forth in Section 75(a) (1-3) of the regulations.

For Advertising Information Contact:
Foxtail Magazine
945 W. Agatite Ave.
Chicago, IL 60640-4044
advertising@foxtailmag.com

FOXTAIL

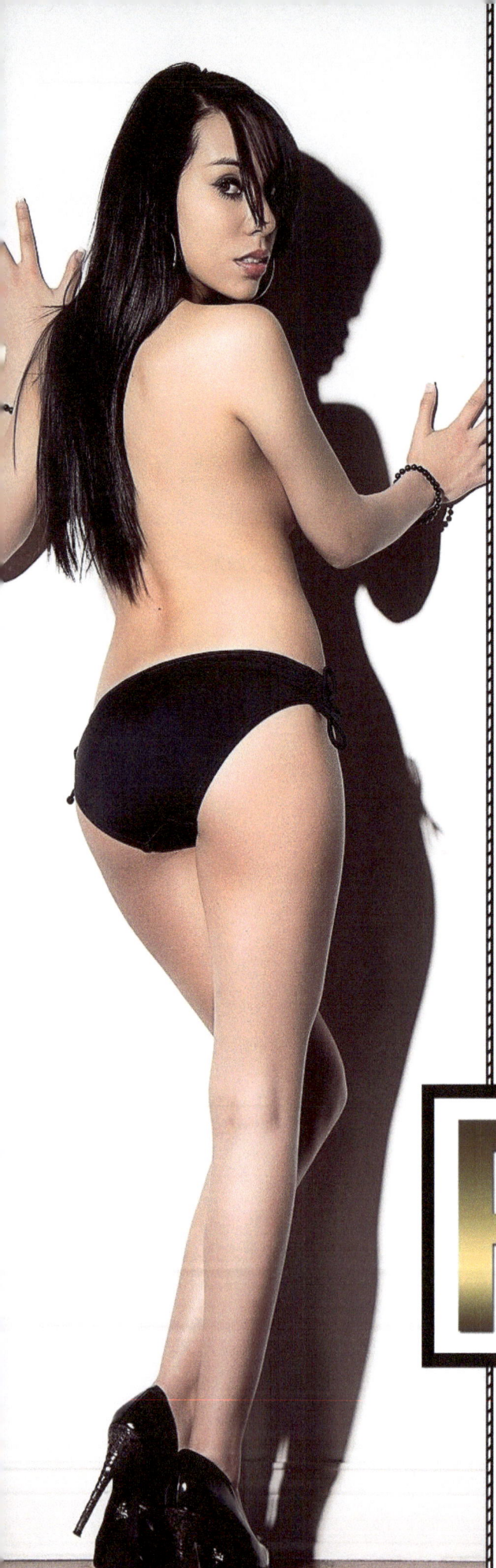

MODEL | JASMINE ALEXANDRA   PG. 24

FOXTAIL MAGAZINE
BEAUTY IS LIFE, AND LIFE IS BEAUTIFUL

EDITOR-IN-CHIEF
Charles C. Rigby II
charles.rigby@foxtailmag.com

ASSISTANT EDITOR
Tony Rudd
tony-rudd@foxtailmag.com

SENIOR PHOTOGRAPHY
Sinovah Kane
sinovakane@gmail.com

GRAPHIC DESIGN/PHOTO EDITING
Sinovah Kane Studios
sinovakane@gmail.com

WRITING STAFF
Erika Jackson
Allura Fox
Jermey Rizner

PHOTOGRAPHY
Martell Jr. Photograpy
@martelljr

Sinovah Kane
@sinovakane

Solomon Abrams

FOXTAIL MAGAZINE

WWW.FOXTAILMAG.COM

CONTACT
info@foxtailmag.com
modeling@foxtailmag.com
submissions@foxtailmag.com

FOXTAIL MAGAZINE

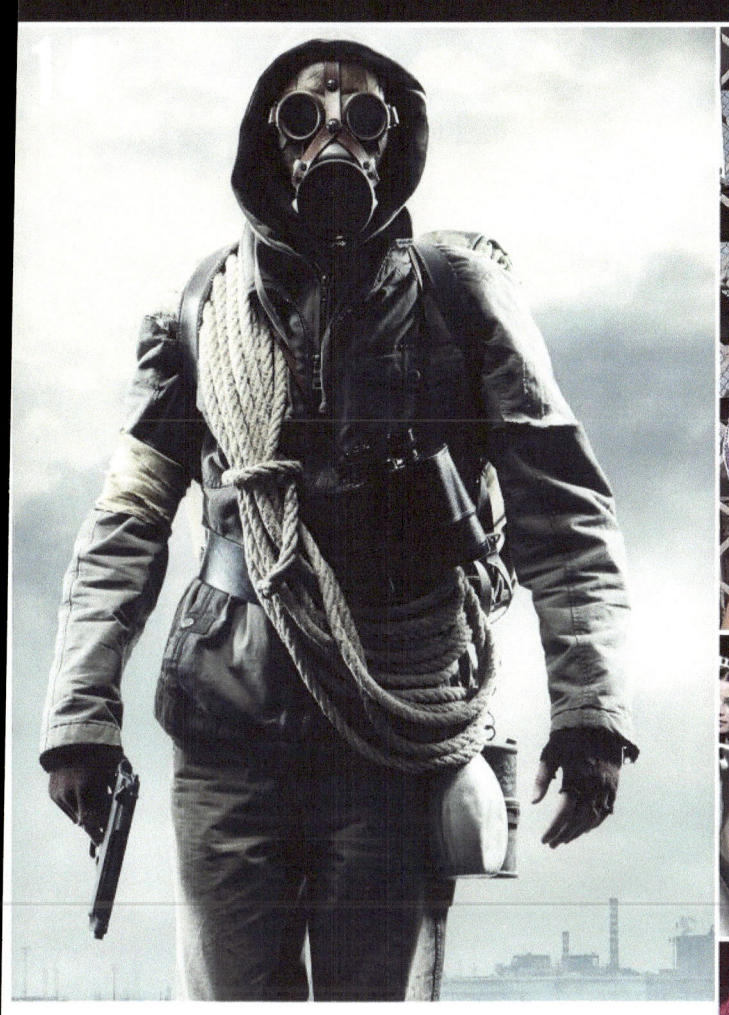

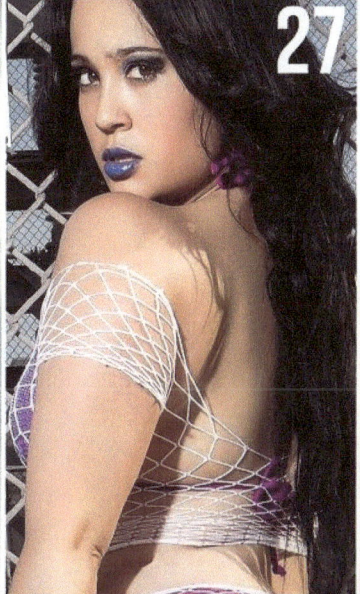
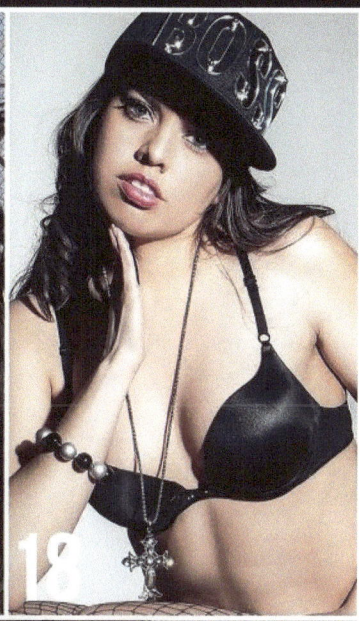
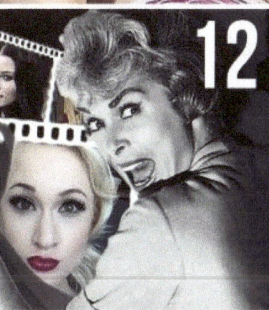
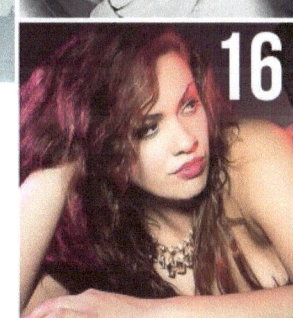
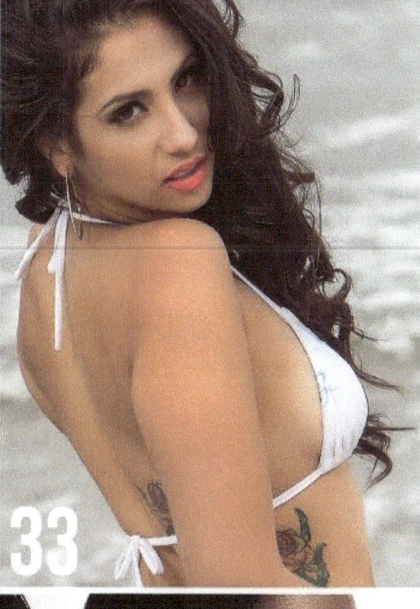
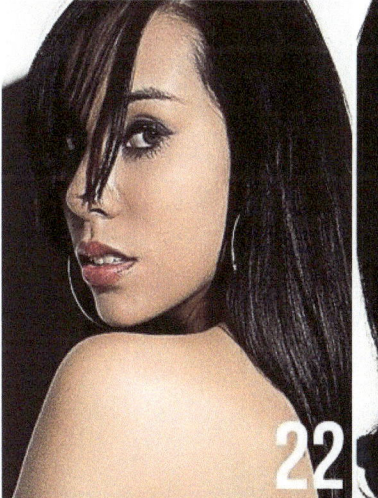
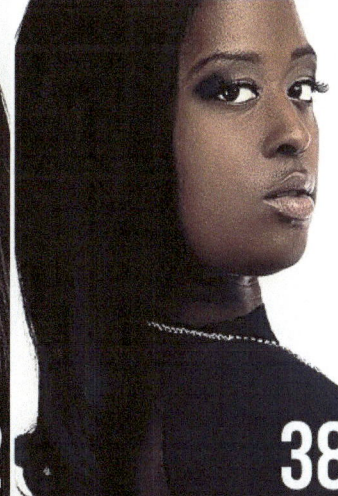

FEATURED ARTICLES

JUN CAI	09
SUPERSTAR DEFENSE	10
PYSCHO/HOTTIE DATING SCALE	11
THE FAPPENING	12
WHEN SHIT HITS THE FAN	14
BELLA VANDALA	16

FEATURED MODELS

DUTCHESS OF CHICAGO	18
JASMINE ALEXANDRA	22
JOLE DACOSTA	27
PRETTY CINDY	33
COCO THE DON	38

I AM
3230

(708) 557-3230 • WWW.IAM3230.COM

SPOTLIGHT: JUN CAI

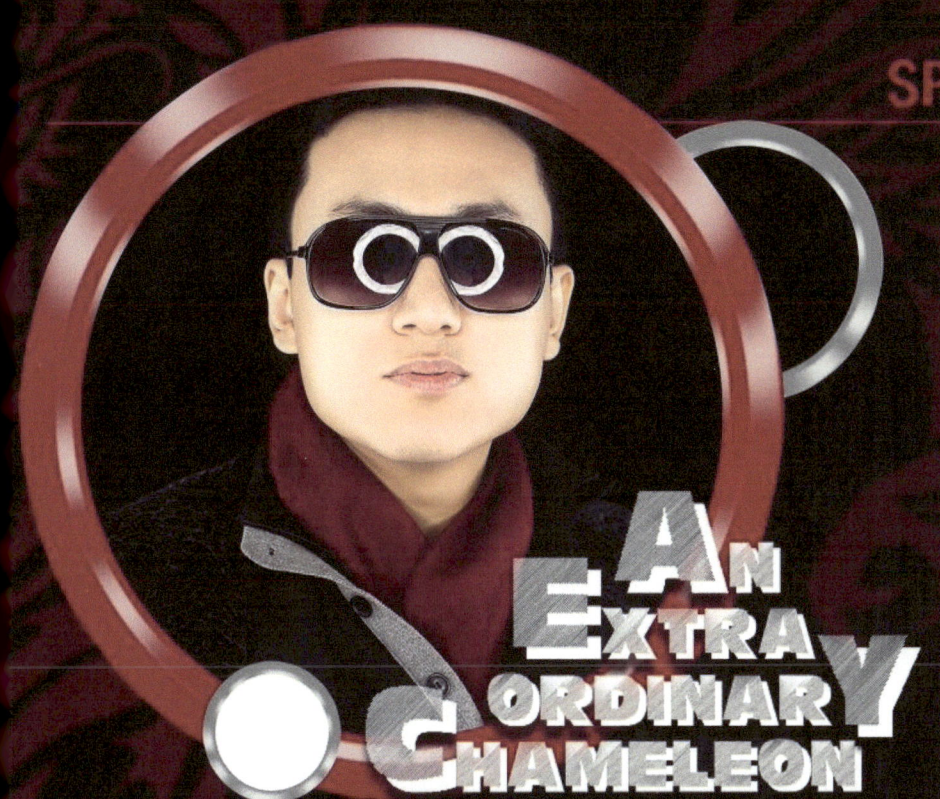

An Extraordinary Chameleon
by Erica D. Jackson

As early as Chris Clark (Motown's first Caucasian R&B artist) and Teena Marie to Robin Thicke and Jon B, music exhibits that soul knows no color. Even when Bobby Caldwell asked "What We Won't Do For Love"; Hall & Oates wanted that "One On One" time. Allow me to entice your musical pallets with the sounds of Jun Cai.

WHEW!! Let me tell you this, I've listened to his music and this multi-talented artist is a driven, passionate force on the grind. Just to warn you, his expertise is FAR past the norm. Just like all of the amazing art, culture and history the beautiful country of China provides, if you open your mind to what this young self-made individual can you show you, trust me, you'll be blown away!

EDJ/FTM: Thank you for the interview. I know you're busy. Please let me say I love your music. It's soulful, I can listen to it everyday. So let's get to know the man behind it.

JC: Well, I'm originally from China (I still have family there). I moved here when I started high school.

EDJ/FTM: How did you get started with music?

JC: Before music, I attended Washington University in St. Louis; majored in Pre-Med Finance and Performing Arts.

EDJ/FTM: REALLY?

JC: Yeah, so I have a business mind and I danced ballet, jazz, Hip Hop, African; even performed off Broadway.

EDJ/FTM: Okay...I am BEYOND way impressed. So how did singing come into play?

JC: I went home in 2012, and in Asia, karaoke is real popular. I'm flipping through the songbook and I come across Ne-Yo and Usher. Now in my country, they really only know Michael Jackson and Justin Timberlake. So someone asked me, "You know how to sing Black music"? Right then, in addition to the inspiration behind my song, "Last Time" made me take singing seriously. I figure if I'm going to do it, then I might as well do it right. So I got voice coaches for R&B and Classical. I really wanted to make sure I went in full throttle. So I figure if I could bridge the cultural gap, then they can relate to more "Black Music" than Michael Jackson and Justin Timberlake.

EDJ/FTM: So where does your drive come from? Do you know what the initial artistic fire is that got you started?

JC: Well.... dancers don't get the recognition in the magnitude of singers. Honestly, having been a dancer, I believe it is the hardest form of art. Your body has to be in its finest form, almost like as an athlete. Even the calisthenics of it makes it necessary. You also need to establish an even balance between art and entertainment, which I'm sure I have acquired. So my diligence and hard work from the point of dance is where it first started.

EDJ/FTM: Do you think the African American culture will embrace your music? Speaking from my generation and the generation behind me?

JC: That's a very good question. I honestly think it's going to be an uphill battle, not because of the content of my music, but because I'm Asian. I feel like I have a responsibility to my people, to break the mold of stereotypes that we face. I mean come on, America looks at Asian women as desirable, exotic. But when they look at the men, they see a caricature. That's how they see us. The industry is what it is, and isn't what it used to be.

EDJ/FTM: Where do you see yourself in five years compared to five years ago?

JC: Well... I have to say I'm really blessed. Straight out of college I worked for J.P. Morgan Chase for a couple years then didn't work for seven. I delved into real estate, investments and I just recently bought a car dealership. I haven't really worked a day in my life. I also have my own production company. I finance my own projects. So just to be able to do what I love and do it well. Being able to pay people is just the making for a wonderful life. So in five years? Whatever happens, happens. I'm blessed now.

EDJ/FTM: It sounds like you are making moves. . . so does that mean your new audience of listeners will have to come to St. Louis to see you perform? Or will you be coming to the CHI soon? What else do you do?

JC: Well no, I am working on some projects, I just want to make sure the right time, venues, shows are aligning right. I have had the opportunity to have my managerial hat on as well.

EDJ/FTM: Really? So you've managed some acts?

JC: Yeah. You know that song "Every Body In The Club Getting Tipsy"? Well J-Kwon is like a little brother to me. So I played a hand in that.

EDJ/FTM: So what are you looking to achieve in the industry?

JC: Well... to be able to have the headline "The First Asian R&B Sensation just signed with Universal Records". But be locked into a six-album deal, honestly, even if I get half the notoriety here in the industry, on the other side of the world, is a whole other market. Basically, people that all look like me... That's mostly where your focus should be is on marketing... making sure it gets to the right media outlet, etc.

EDJ/FTM: Well...to say I am looking forward to your future endeavors is an understatement. I wish you well...and again thank you for the interview.

JC: Thank you!

Well.... there you have it. The next Asian R&B break-out artist. Jun Cai. TRUST me...GET IN TUNE

IN THE GAME | *Where You Need To Be*

Have "Da Bears" Found Their Next Superstar on Defense?

By Jeremy Rizner

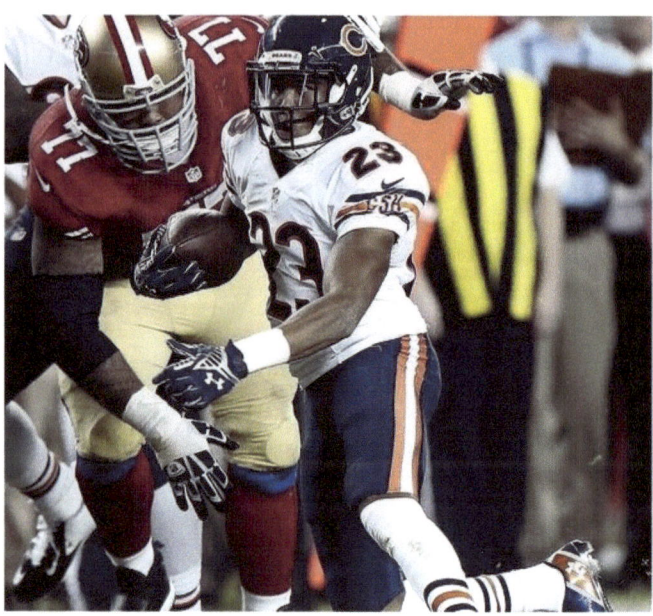

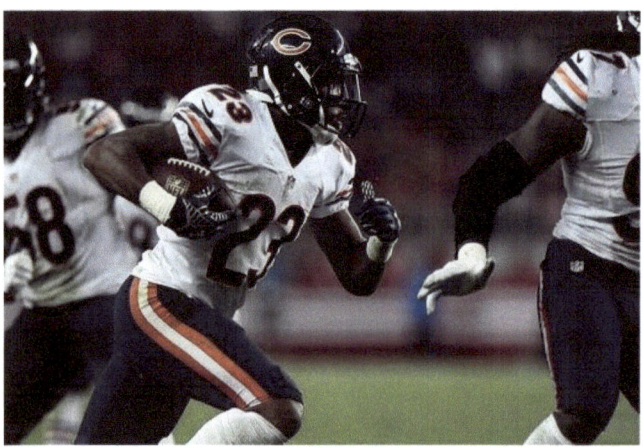

The Bears end the first quarter of the season with a 3-4 record (0-3 at home and 4-0 on the road) and are in third place behind the Green Bay Packers (5-2) and division leading Detroit Lions (5-2). The Bears have looked inconsistent on both sides of the ball, but the defense didn't have many expectations from fans and insiders. The defense was supposed to be better with all of the offseason moves geared towards helping the defense. The shining light at the end of the tunnel might be our first round draft pick, Kyle Fuller.

Fuller is a 22 year old 6'0" tall cornerback out of the University of Virginia Tech. He was selected by the Bears with pick #14 in the first round of the 2014 NFL Draft (side note: the NFL has just decided to have the 2015 NFL Draft in Chicago). This was yet another not well received Phil Emery first round pick by fans, but most analysts thought it was a reach on Fuller. He was a pick for the future since most Bears personnel and insiders thought this was going to be Charles "Peanut" Tillman's last season with the Bears.

Fast forward to week two against the 49ers and Tillman ends up hurting the same forearm that plagued him last year and made him miss the final six games of last season. With Tillman out, it was Fuller's time to shine in a primetime game on Sunday Night Football.

Shine he did. Fuller started by picking off Colin Kapernick Quarterback of the 49ers twice and helped the Bears with a comeback victory 28-20. Next game for the Bears was another primetime matchup against the Jets on Monday Night Football. Fuller followed his amazing game against the Niners with another great performance with an interception and two forced fumbles to help the Bears win 27-19 and moving the Bears to 2-1.

With these performances, Fuller was able to win some accolades: NFC week 2 defensive player of the week (2014) & NFL week 3 defensive rookie of the week (2014). This past week, though Fuller did get to come back to reality a little bit with a thrashing at the hands of Aaron Rodgers Quarterback of the Green Bay Packers, he went 22-28 for 302 yards and 4 TD's and zero interceptions. The pass rush was non-existent but we also did finally get to see Fuller look like a rookie in this game that the Bears lost 38-17 and fell to 2-2.

Even with that performance against Green Bay, Fuller still was able to be named NFC defensive rookie of the month (Sep. 2014) and his stats so far look like this through four games: 22 total tackles, 3 Interceptions, 2 forced fumbles, and 4 passes deflected. Fuller was also the first player in the last 20 seasons to record three interceptions and two forced fumbles in their first three games. I can't predict the future nor am I good at guessing it, but Bears fans, let's give Phil Emery a silent clap and head nod because he might have found another gem in the first round like he did with Kyle Long in the 2013 NFL Draft. As with Long, Fuller was not a fan favorite when the draft happened, but his play has spoken for itself. Emery also looks like he might have found a key piece in Fuller to get this defense back to being the monsters of the midway!

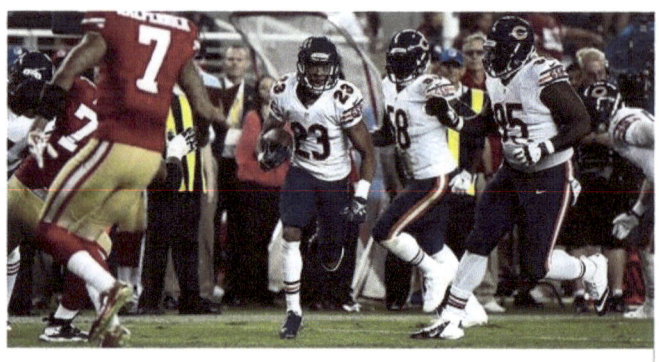

SEX & RELATIONSHIPS

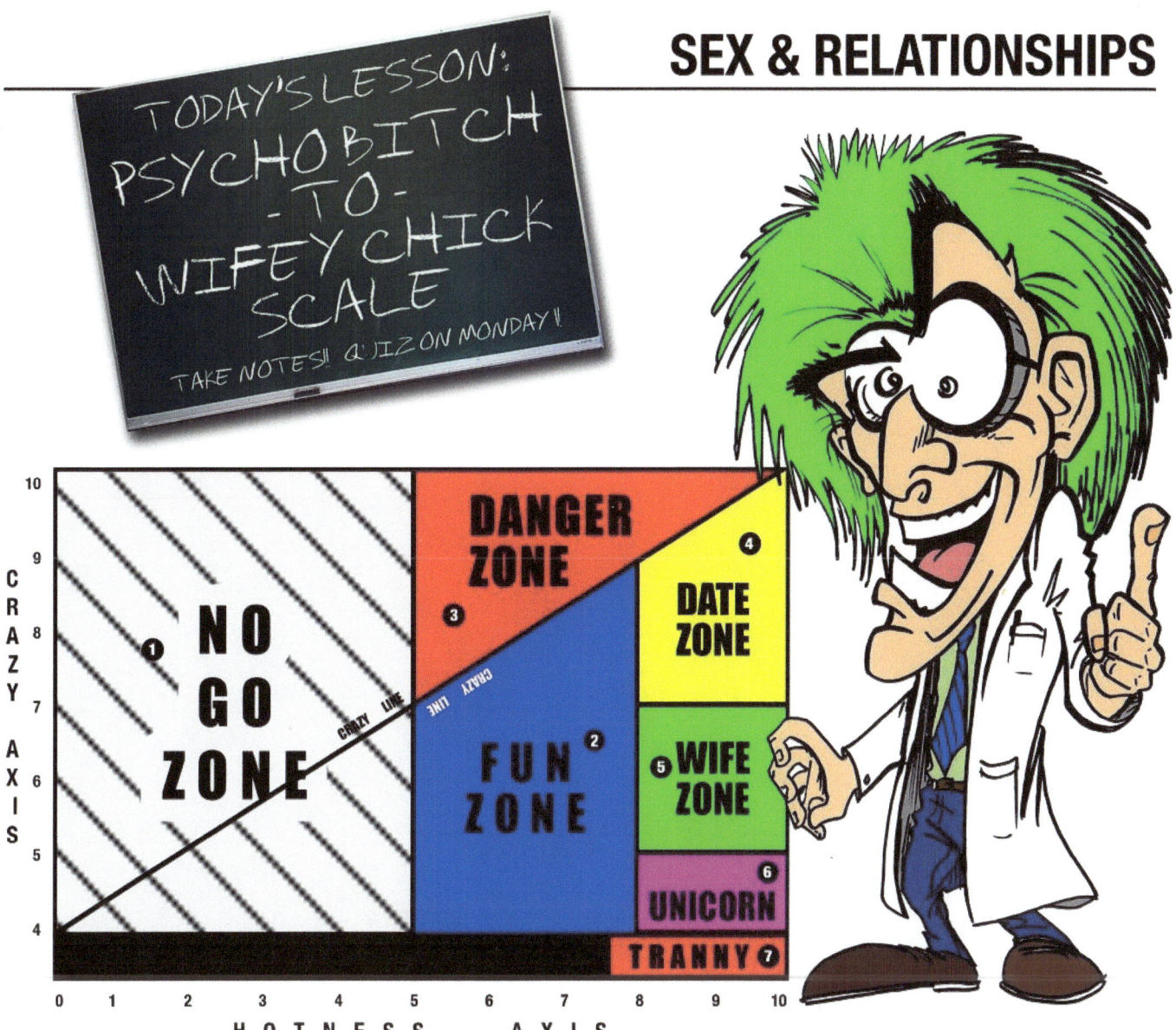

The Universal Hot/Crazy scale is everything a young man need to know about a woman.

HOW IT WORKS

The chart is seperated by a "**Crazy Axis**" and a "**Hot Axis**". We measure hotness from 0 to 10. We measure crazy from 4 to 10 because there is no such thing as a woman that's not at least level 4 crazy.

The line through the middle of the graph is your crazy line.

NO GO ZONE ❶

As a rule, 0 to 5 on the hot axis is the "No Go Zone". You never waste time hanging out and dating women that you consider to be less than a 5. You don't go there. Life is better this way. That's just the way it is…

FUN ZONE ❷

Between a 5 and 8 on the Hot Axis and below the crazy line is your "Fun Zone". You can hang out and spend time with women in this area. When you're in the fun zone, keep in mind that you want to move out of the fun zone and into a more permanent relationship as soon as possilbe.

DANGER ZONE ❸

Above the crazy line, we have the "Danger Zone". These are your red heads (real or fake), strippers, bartenders, hair dressers, girls name Unique, and baby mamas. This is where you get cars keyed, unplanned pregnancies, tire slashing, and jail time. You want to stay clear of women that fall in the danger zone.

Remeber: This is not a static environment. You must use this scale over time to develop reliable data. Because any woman can appear anywhere on this chart, and eventually slip into the danger zone at any time. So really, you want to collect data over a group of experiences and formulate an astute opinion once you have collect sufficient data.

DATE ZONE ❹

Below the crazy line, above 8 on the hot axis, but still about a 7 on the crazy is your date zone. You can stay in the date zone forever. These are women you introduce to friends and family. They're good looking and reason able not crazy most of the time.

WIFE ZONE ❺

Above an 8 on the hot axis, and between a 7 and 5 on the crazy axis is your, "Wife Zone". When you meet this girl, you should consider a long term relationship. This is where you want to be. You're looking for a woman that fall into this area 90% of the time during the course of your relationship.

UNICORN ZONE ❻

Now! Below a 5 crazy and between an 8 and 10 on the hot axis is your "Unicorn Zone". These things simply don't exist. If you find a unicorn, please capture her safely. Keep her alive. We'd like to study her, and possibly replicate her.

IT'S A MAN ❼

Lastly, if you meet a girl that is between 9 and 10 on the hot axis, and a 2 or 3 on the crazy axis, process with caution! This is a dude, and you're talking to a tranny!

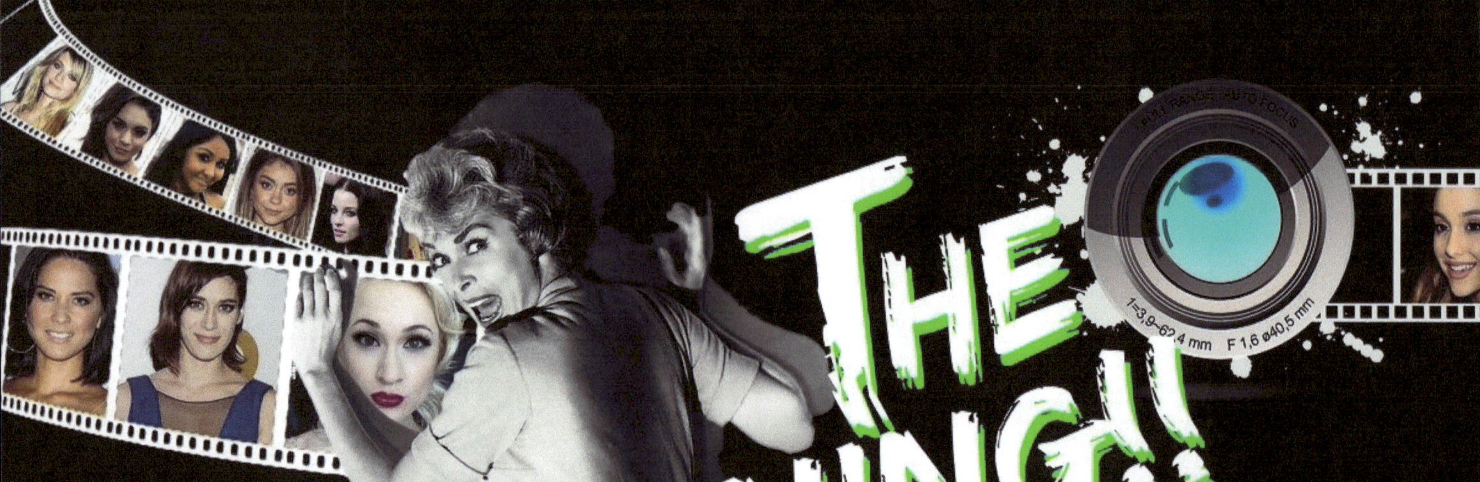

The Fappening!!

The Scariest Moment in Hollywood Since the Start of TMZ!!

It's likely origin is British, their equivalent to jack off, but it was definitely popularized for the entire English-speaking world by the online community reddit as its de facto term for masturbation. And of course, a happening is an event.

DISCLAIMER: FOXTAIL Magazine doesn't condone or support the illegal hacking of private information, pictures, or videos. We, also, do not support the "slut-shamming" of women (celebrity or otherwise) whose only crime is partaking in a private social activity commit by millions people (both men and women) around the world. However... We do believe that if you decide to take a selfie. And if you decide to take a selfie in the nude. And if you decide to take a selfie in the nude on a cellphone. And if you decide to take a selfie in the nude on a cellphone and share it to iCloud. Then, you need to take some responsiblity and accept that there maybe some dire consequences that come along with that decision.

An Overview of "The Fappening"

As many of you might already know, there has been a breach in celebrity privacy recently, which unveiled hundreds of nude pictures of a lot of celebrities which supposedly used their iPhones to take the personal pictures. The Fappening has had a total of 3 total leaks as of October, 2014 the sheer amount of photos leaked are not all confirmed, but they're supposedly valid, at least in their vast majority. However, given the popularity of the trend, there's already speculation that forged pictures and older nudes have been released (or re-released, respectively) as part of the trend.

Why Do They Call It "The Fappening"?

The word fappening is a portmanteau of fap and happening, similar to words like Sharknado or Thanksgivukkah, or more conventionally smog. Fap is an onomatopoeiatic word, a word that sounds like the thing it's representing, like boom, splat or click. The thing fap refers to is masturbating and I'll let your imagination connect the auditory dots there.

How and Why The Fappening Started

The first official pictures were posted on image sharing site 4chan. From there, they spread to Tumblr, Imgur and even Reddit. The first batch was posted on August 31st, 2014 and users had to pay the leaker in Bitcoins to get access to them. Many now believe that the photos circulated the web at least two weeks prior to them being first officially posted on a popular platform.

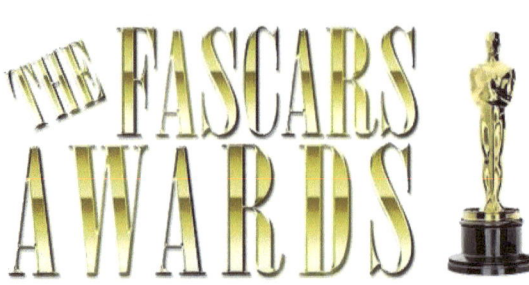

THE FASCARS AWARDS

"BEST VIDEO"
Abigail Spencer
Her nickname should be "The Flicker".

"MOST PISSED"
Jennifer Lawrence
Don't fuck with Jenny Law!

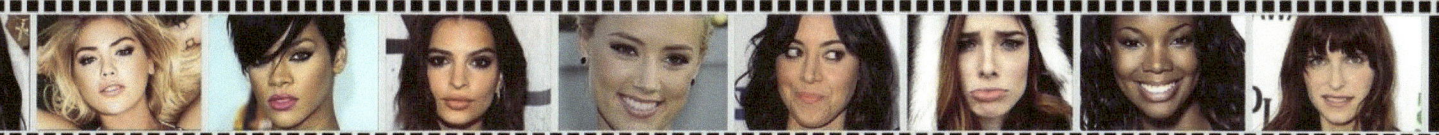

There were two subreddits on Reddit which were dedicated to the posting of associated naked pictures. Both of them have been removed as they posed problems for administrators who were assaulted by the community for allowing the subreddits.

The pictures were allegedly obtained by hackers who targeted the accounts of the celebs in question. Apple has denied that its cloud servers have been breached, stating that it's more likely that individual accounts have been targeted through phishing tactics or brute-force guessing of passwords and login credentials. However, there is no clear statement released by authorities investigating the issue, so it's safe to say that Apple might just be blaming hackers instead of admitting to some vulnerability in their services.

Now, as far as I'm concerned, this whole thing could have been easily avoided by using two-step authentication methods offered by Apple to its users. Also, everybody should be aware that the pictures they take with their iPhones are automatically uploaded to the cloud. While I don't personally believe that Apple employees have access to said servers, why take the risk altogether? Simply stop the automatic upload of pictures to the iCloud and store them on a personal computer or device if you don't want them on your phone.

But truth be told, while I don't condone the behavior and decisions of the hackers who distributed the pictures, they knew they were going to make some money from it. The rest of people who distributed them are just after the popularity that comes with having access to and distributing nude photos of celebs. I don't think it's something personal someone had with any celebrity targeted by the hackers – but I do strongly believe that the fault rests on both Apple and the celebrities themselves. While I understand the need for privacy and all that, why on earth would you take nude pictures of yourself? Don't you know how easy it is for you to lose your phone, or as in this case, get your account hacked? With all the public attention you're getting, why risk it?

Everybody is entitled to their own privacy and I hate it when the media goes after the silliest little thing in order to sell something. But when you're taking up a public image, it comes with a whole lot of responsibility. And what people fail to understand is that technology may be apt in keeping your private data safe, it's not foolproof. Maybe this will be the wakeup call for most.

Until now, there have been a number of celebs, including Kim Kardashian, Rihanna, Amber Heard, Jennifer Lawrence, Nicki Minaj, Scarlett Johansson, Rachel Nichols, Hayden Panettierre, Mary-Kate Olsen and Kate Upton, to name but a few. For the time being, mostly female celebrities were targeted, while male celebs are fearing their turn might come soon as well and are taking precautions to protect their accounts. A bunch of female celebs are suing Google for $100 million because the search giant has allegedly ignored requests to delete the pictures from platforms it operates, such as YouTube and Blogger.

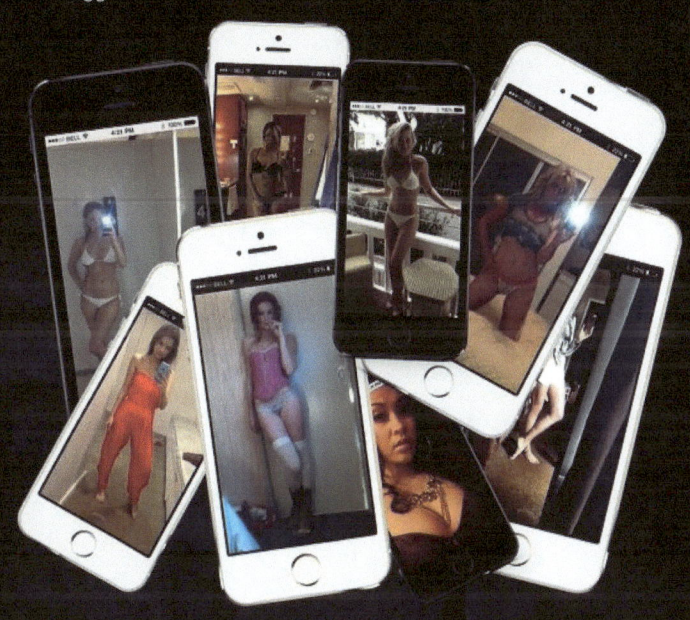

"MOST UNECESSARY"
Rihanna
Who hasn't seen Rihanna naked, lol.

"MOST SELFIES"
Amber Heard
Johnny Deep is a real lucky guy!

"MOST CREEPY"
Sarah Hyland
Seriously Hackers? Seriously? SMDH!

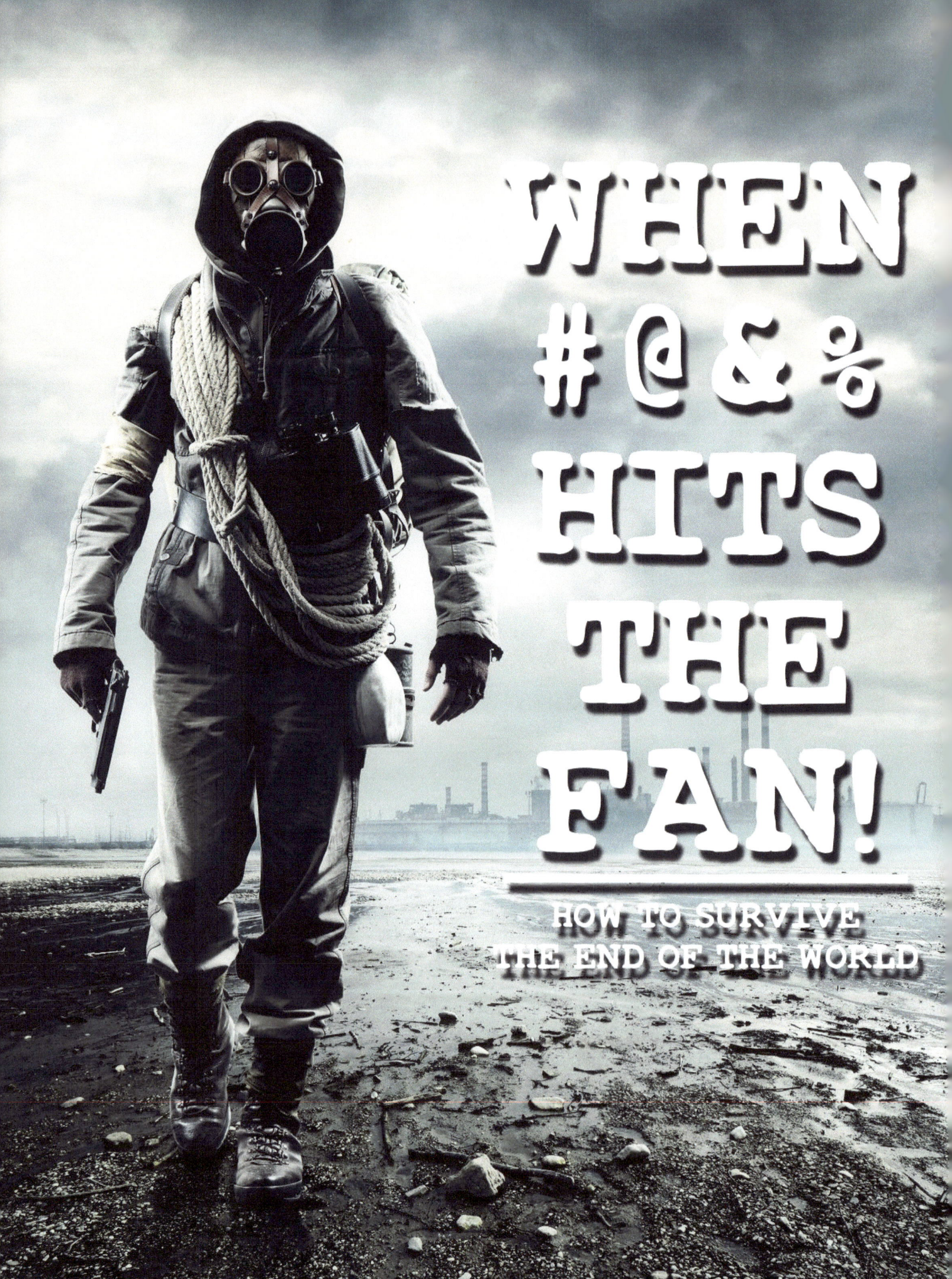

WHEN THE #@&% HITS THE FAN!

Technology has evolved tremendously in the last century and it's a little scary to think what will happen in the next few decades. Let's face it, two decades ago we didn't know anything about smartphones. Now, there is literally an app for everything. Technology is not the only thing that has changed over the years. Our economy dramatically worsened year after year. Small wars tranform into genocide and bloodshed. Human society rests on the brink of a global meltdown and you need to know a few things.

With the overall situation worsening and becoming more and more unpredictable, preparing for doomsday might actually be a really important thing to do. An infinite number of global tragic events can occur at any moment. Some of the more commonly feared events include: total economic collapse, nuclear-level EMP attacks, catastrophic climate change like earthquakes, tornadoes or solar flares.

Of course, each situation needs to be treated and addressed in a different way. Despite various specifics, overall doomsday scenarios always require a standard collection of proper equipment. The right tools and devices could mean the difference between life and death.

In case of an economic catastrophe, you need to prepare yourself with gallons of water, canned food, gasoline, flashlights, and batteries as well as some cutting tools. As any of these are very important, the latter can be used to create useful weapons that might come in handy if you want to set up and defend your base. A medical kit is always crucial in your battle for survival.

Nuclear attacks mean that you will have to stay underground. This basically will require continuous source of lights, so flashlights and a generator are very important. Creating a bunker with solar panels might be really useful here as it can help you transform solar power into light and heat.

Food is also critical, as well as some basic tools such as hammers; especially, if you want to build something underground with the materials at your disposal.

In case of a natural disaster, such as a tornado, you need to make sure that you always have on you the most important items; these should be fitted in a backpack. A knife, med kit, compass, a fire starting kit, some food that can last for a long time, particularly canned food, as well as some water and a blanket.

Of course, you can prepare an even larger kit with more items, but such a kit is easier to carry in a backpack as you try to avoid any disasters that might come your way. Things like water filtration, starting a fire, and finding a shelter are crucial because without them your body temperature will start dropping fast and if the water isn't safe, you will face lots of diseases.

Solar flares are also a very dark scenario, because if they do happen, they will literally wipe out all communication on Earth, so we won't be able to talk with each other if we are located at a large distance. We don't need to panic, instead we have to focus on the matter at hand and use the car or some other means of transportation to get to other people. In this state of worldwide panic, you must be careful, because people can get very territorial. Take blankets, food, water and many of the items portrayed in the natural disaster scenario.

As you can see, these doomsday scenarios might become more real than you can imagine really soon, so it's crucial to ensure that you are geared properly. Having the proper gear and food can certainly make the difference, so prepare yourself for the worst. You will certainly feel a lot better in these dramatic situations.

WRITTEN BY: DONNOVAN86

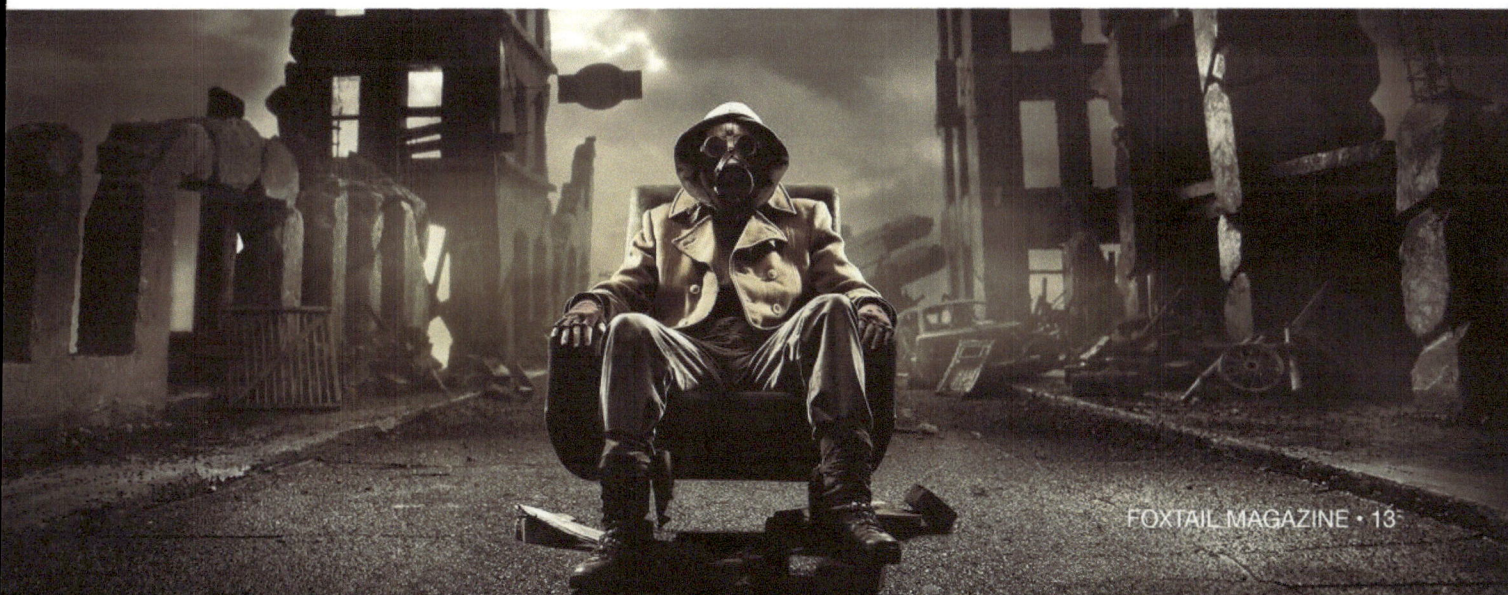

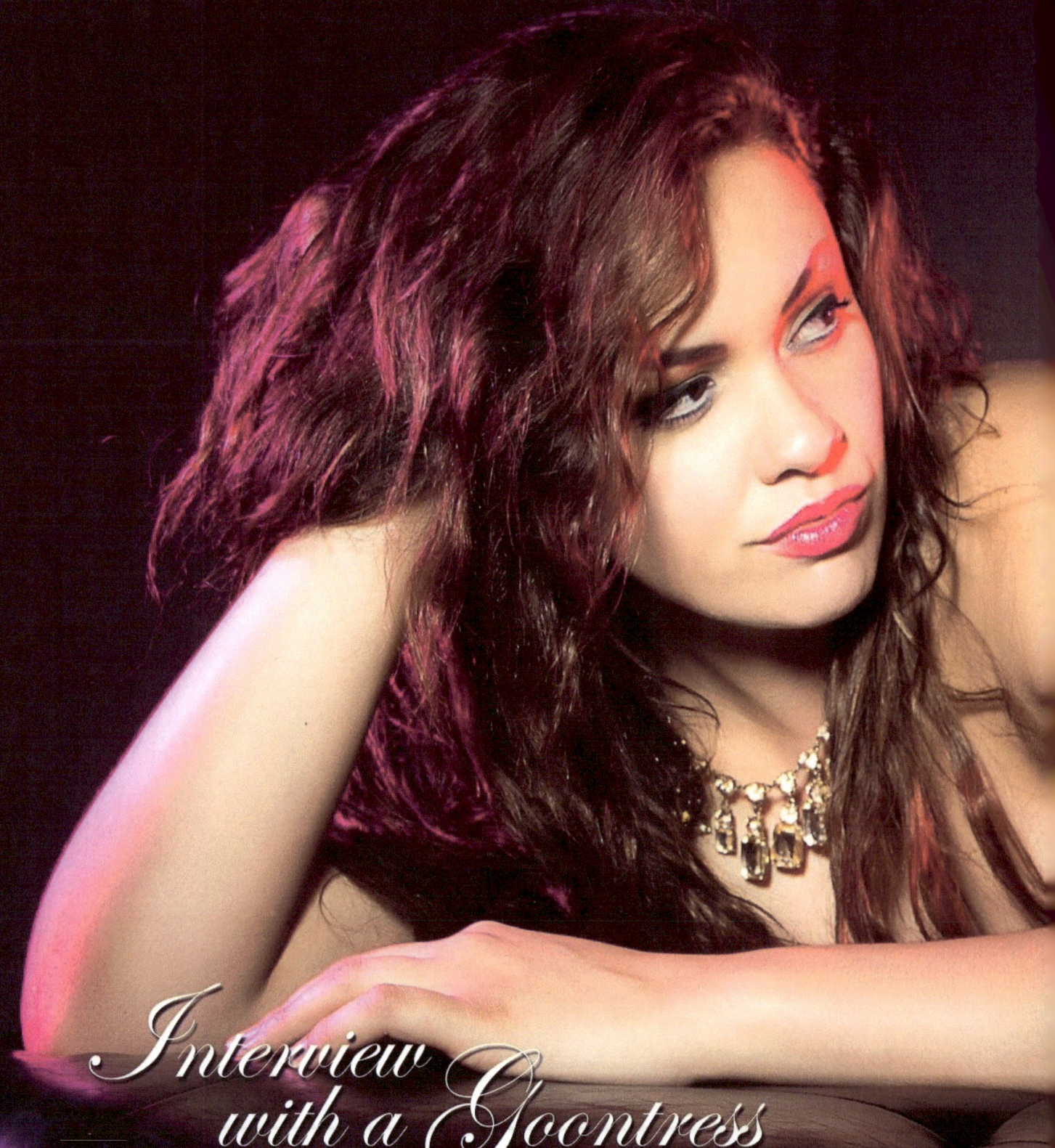

INTERVIEW WITH A GOONTRESS: BELLA VANDALA

FTM: Where are you from?

BV: Chicago, Illinois, Northwest side. Originally my family is from Logan Square, first generation born in America and I've moved around ever since I was a kid. Basically, I've lived a little bit of everywhere, suburbs, city, and country.

FTM: What are your thoughts on the current state of the game?

BV: It's kind of depressing. How can I word this without insulting anybody? It's all very fake. And it's hard to remain real when the biggest opportunity for you to make millions in your life consists with dealing with fake people on a regular basis. That's why I say it's depressing, because it's almost like you do have to sell a certain piece of yourself in order to operate in this game.

FTM: Ok, who would you say influenced your style?

BV: Lil' Kim. I was a huge Lil' Kim fan. I think Aliyah influenced me the most dancing with my dance career. And it was definitely Lil' Kim that influenced me with the rap, the raunchy, real gutty, primarily from your throat and your stomach, that hard core shit. I loved her because she was gangster glam. And I was so obsessed with it when I was younger. I fucks with Nikki, I really do, I like her because she's bold, she's different, she's obnoxious, she's rude and she is a gimmick.

FTM: In femcee history, I think most women that make it in the game take on a strong male dominated persona.

BV: You have to. You really have to, because if you're going to target a male demographic which is primarily who promotes and purchases, you have to be identifiable to them, marketable to them and men keep their house bitch in the crib. That's why strippers and all that other shit is the side hoe. It's the arrogant women, it's the 'I don't give a fuck' women.

FTM: The bad girls?

BV: The bad girls!

FTM: I know you're just starting out, but do you have anything that you consider really successful or a high point in your career this far?

BV: I like the "what the fuck" factor. I don't know if I'd say that was a high point in my career. But the look I see on people's face when they listen to my music is always the high point for me. When they hear that I rap or they hear that I make music they think that I'm just some dipsy, dumb white girl who's going to suck. So that look that they get on their face when I'm sitting in front of them and I'm drilling the shit out of a fucking trap beat. That's the high point in my career.

BV: That kind of recognition, first they're all like, 'this bitch!' And then they're like, 'woah, ok the beat drops, maybe this might be worth listening to.' Then they hear the lyrics and they rock on with you. That's always going to be the high point.

FTM: What obstacles have you over come thus far?

BV: Been a white girl rapping. That's a pretty big fucking obstacle to overcome. And being taken seriously in the studio. The advances from all the fake rappers and producers. A lot of people get you in the studio and no matter how talented you are if you aren't fucking, You aren't worth their time. Not having any money to start, that was rough.

FTM: As an artist, especially rap artist. Would you rather go the independent rap?

BV: I would definitely rather go independent than anything, no doubt about it. If I had the funds to invest in myself the way I wanted to I wouldn't work with anybody. I would just do me because I know that that's going to turn the biggest profit. But realistically, with what I'm given I'm going to need some financial backing, an investor, possibly a label. But I will buy myself out and I will go independent.

FTM: What inspires your lyrics?

BV: Real life, things that have happened to me.

FTM: What's your favourite thing to do when you aren't writing, producing, playing? How do you take yourself out of the rap?

BV: Graffiti. And cars. I'm a bit of a gear head.

FTM: That is real. So what kind of music do you listen to other than rap?

BV: I listen to a lot of Spanish music. I love Salsa, I love Cha Cha. I love reggae. I like a lot of 90s Rhythm and Blues.

FTM: You like Jodeci?

BV: Yes, I'm a huge Jodeci fan, Janet Jackson. All that shit.

FTM: This is an off question, but I just thought about it. How would you prefer to be marketed?

BV: Yes.

FTM: So how do you feel about that as a female artist. Is that something you're going to trouble with?

BV: No, I'm very comfortable with my sexuality. Very comfortable. I like being in sexy, I like having sex.

FTM: Definitely, putting that in the article.

BV: I like to say perverse things for shock value quite often, so I'm not opposed to being marketed as sexy. But I think if I had to describe myself it would be like an all American badass girl next door.

FTM: So, just based on a song I listened to, I'm assuming Toppy is what I think it is?

BV: What?

FTM: Toppy?

BV: Oh yes.

FTM: I'm just making sure.

BV: Sloppy with Toppy.

FTM: That's the line.

BV: It's got to be sloppy, if it ain't sloppy it ain't working.

FTM: I should introduce you to a couple of girls I know. Have you performed live?

BV: Yes

FTM: How did it go?

BV: It went well. I got the "oh shit" factor. At first everybody is like 'fuck is this bitch?' And then I'm up there and sometimes I go in a cheerleader's voice, 'Hi! My name is Bella. I'll be rapping tonight!' And then the beat drops and they go, 'Oh what the fuck!'

FTM: That's a great way to introduce yourself, work with that!

BV: It's comedy.

FTM: That will blow people away. I'd be blown away if I saw that myself.

BV: Because they think you're going to flop and they're waiting to laugh and they're automatically smiling and looking at you like this dumb bitch.

FTM: So you got the whole eight mile thing going.

BV: Yes. Nothing's more entertaining than the element of surprise.

FTM: Is there any advice, I hate that question. Is there any advice you would like to give to young aspiring rappers?

BV: Yes, time is working against your dream harder than you will ever work towards them. So every decision you make is critical. Don't hesitate. Don't doubt yourself. Jump down with all of your fucking movement.

#TRENDING_NOW

STAY CONNECTED

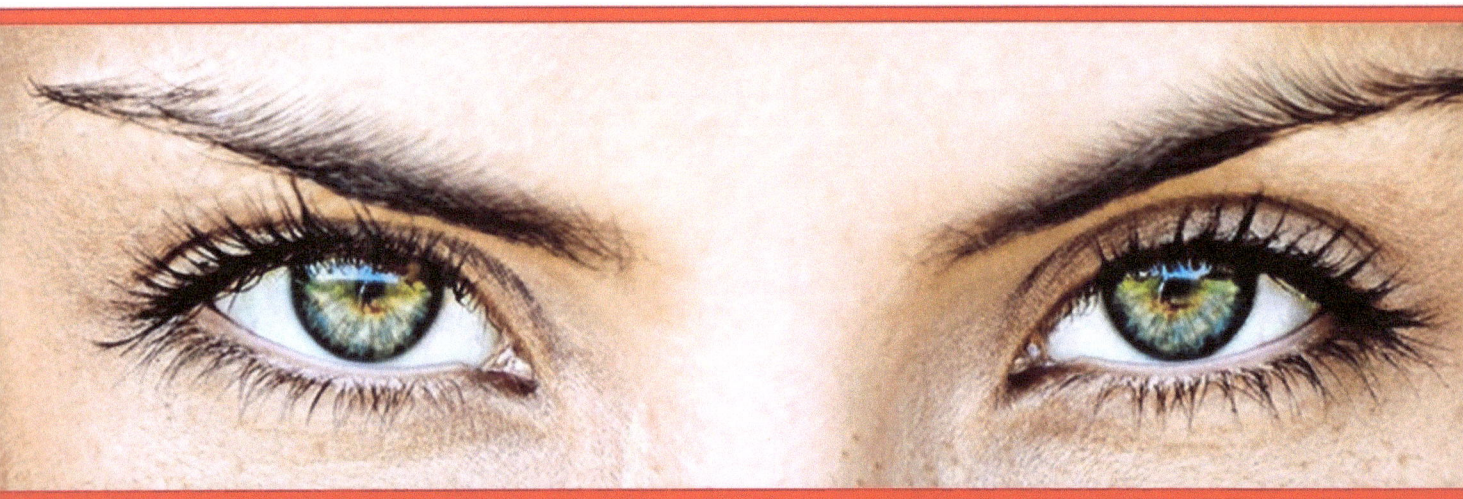

WITH
FOXTAIL MAGAZINE

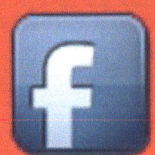 FACEBOOK.COM/FOXTAILMAGAZINE    INSTAGRAM.COM/FOXTAIL_MAGAZINE

 VIMEO.COM/FOXTAILMAGAZINE    TWITTER.COM/FOXTAIL_MAG

FOXTAIL MAGAZINE PRESENT

HOT N' SPICY EDITION

FOXTAILMAG.COM

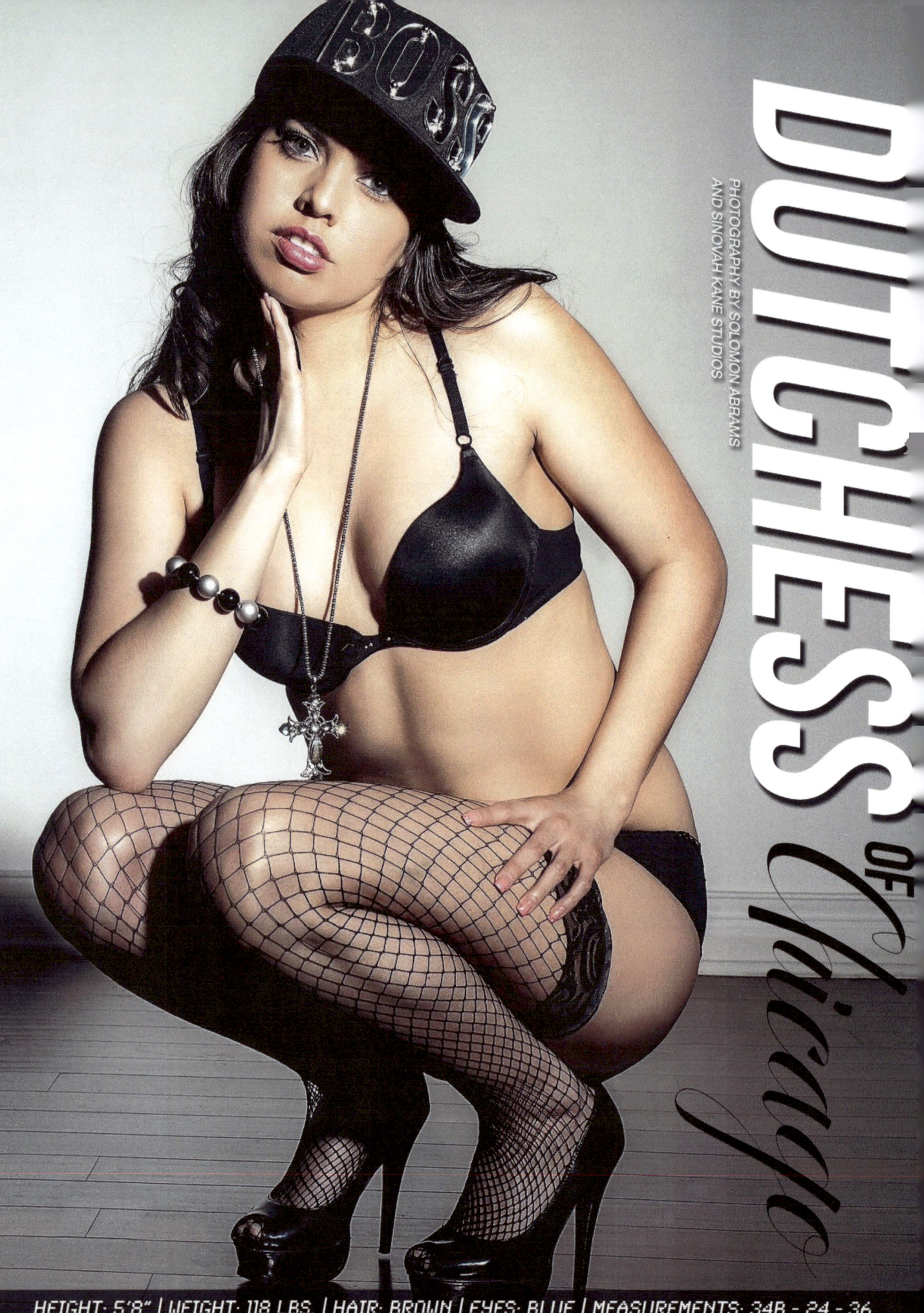

DUTCHESS OF Chicago

PHOTOGRAPHY BY SOLOMON ABRAMS AND SINOVAH KANE STUDIOS

HEIGHT: 5'8" | WEIGHT: 118 LBS. | HAIR: BROWN | EYES: BLUE | MEASUREMENTS: 34B - 24 - 36

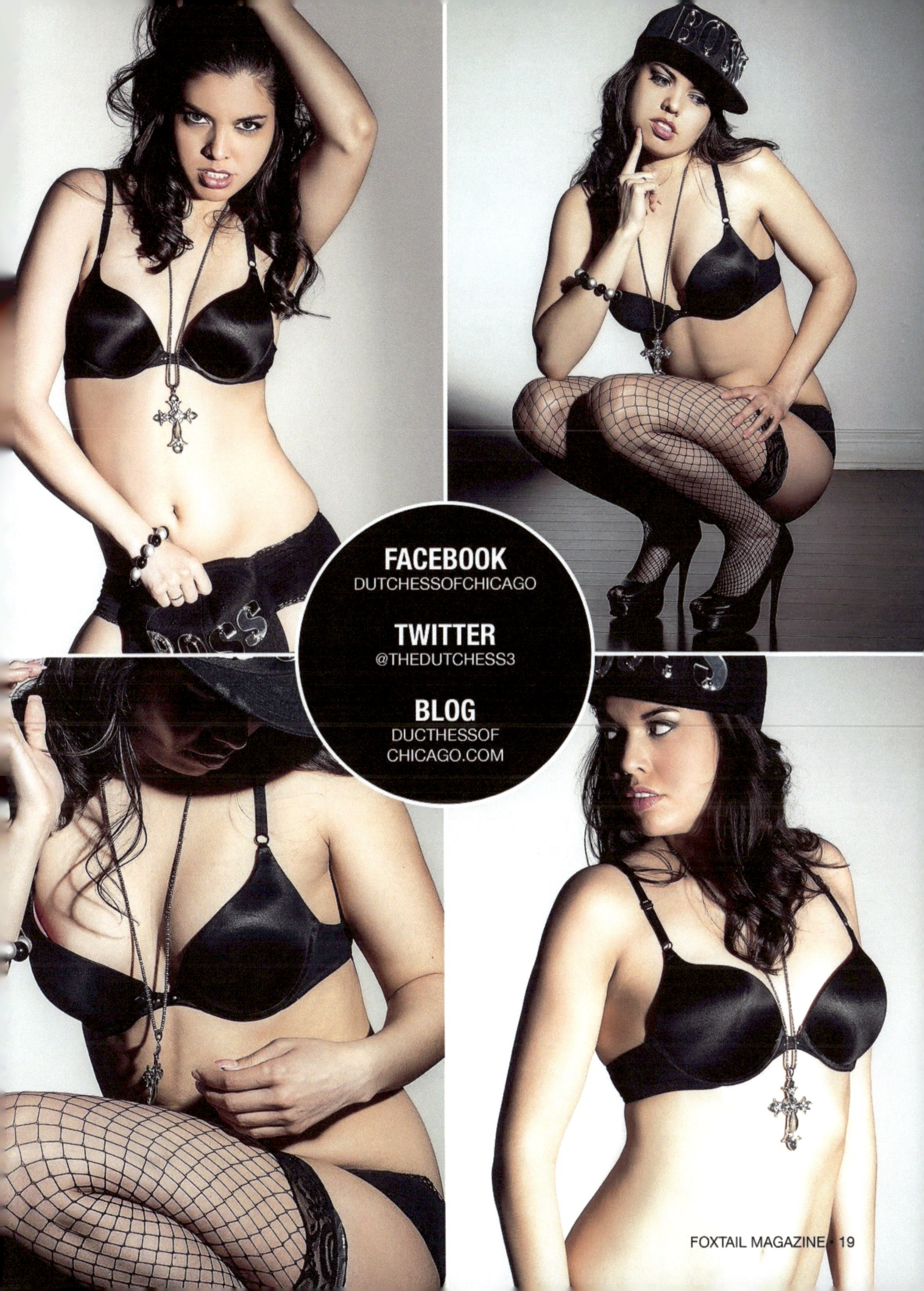

DUCTHESS OF CHICAGO

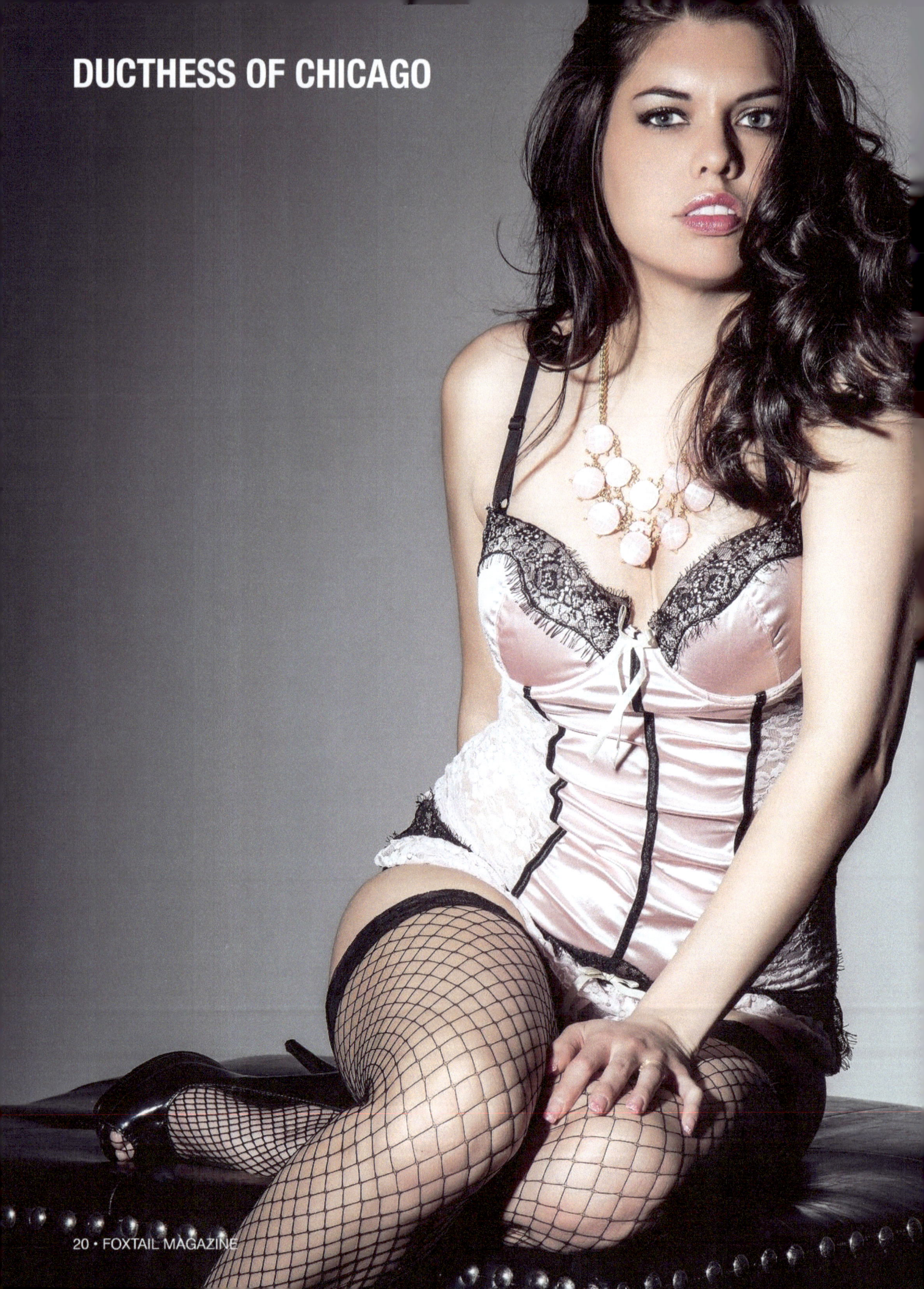

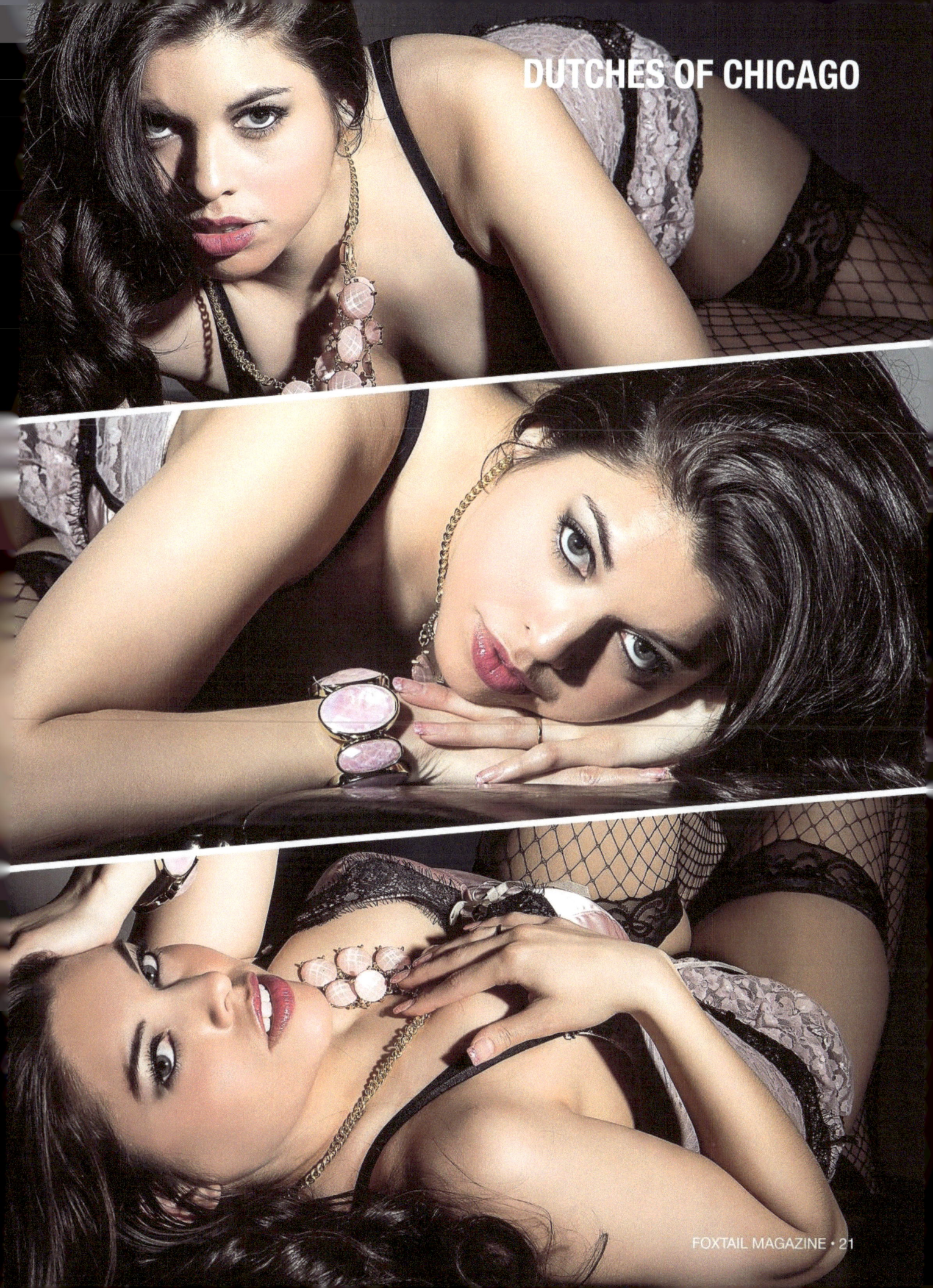

JASMINE *Alexandria*

PHOTOS BY SINOVAH KANE PHOTOGRAPHY

HEIGHT: 5'6" | WEIGHT: 110 LBS. | HAIR: BLACK | EYES: BROWN | MEASUREMENTS: 34B - 26 - 36

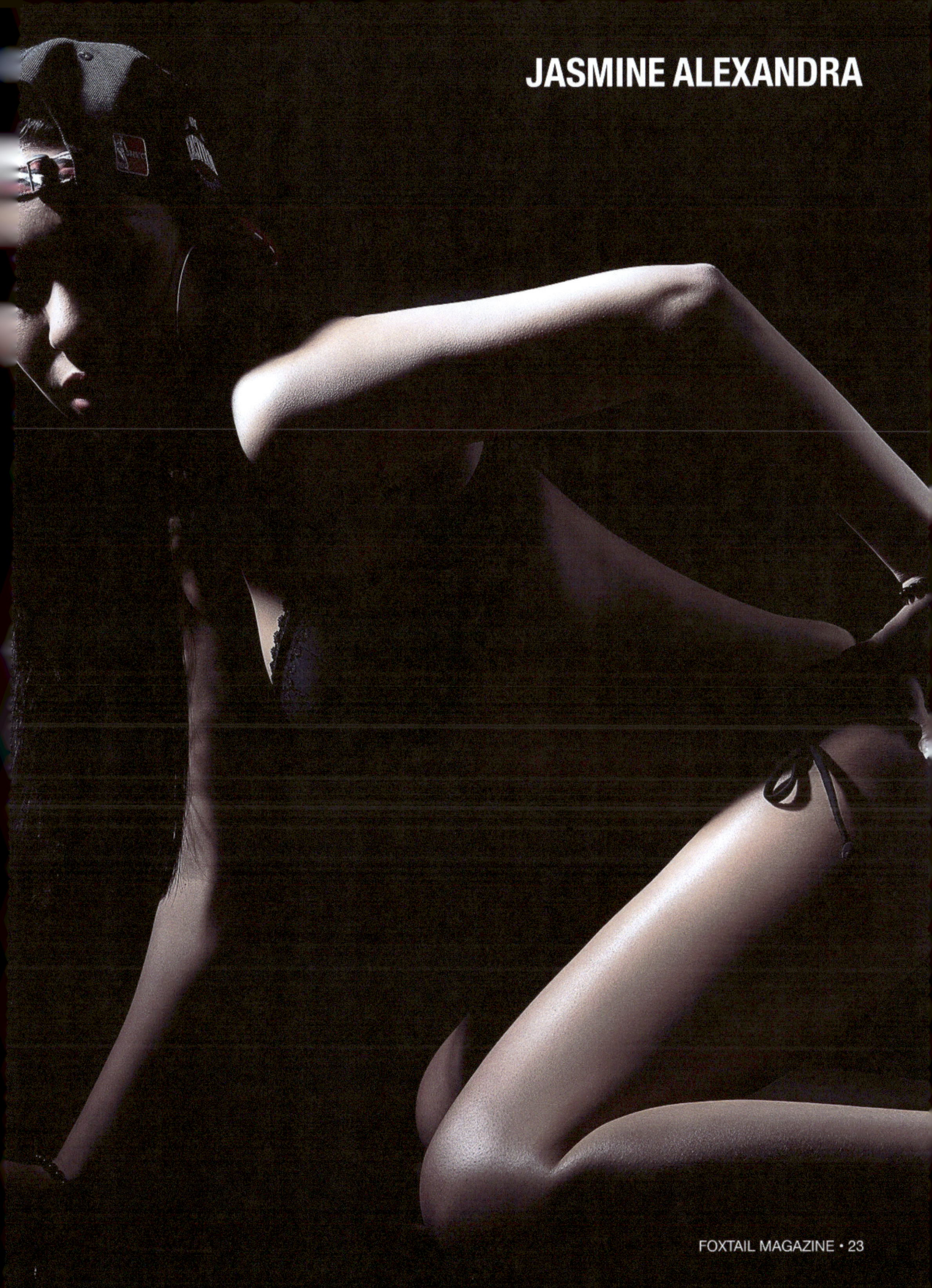

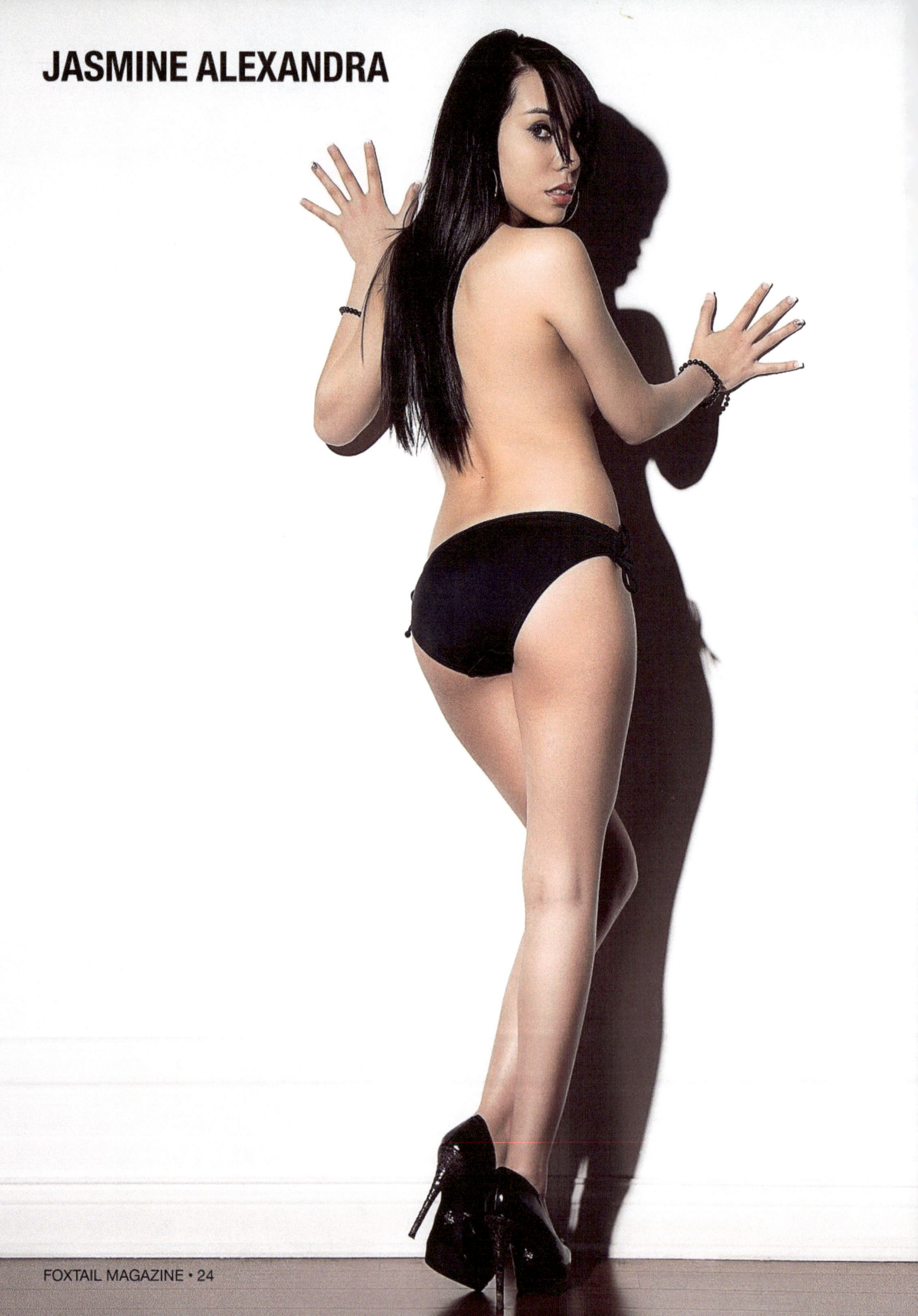

JASMINE ALEXANDRA

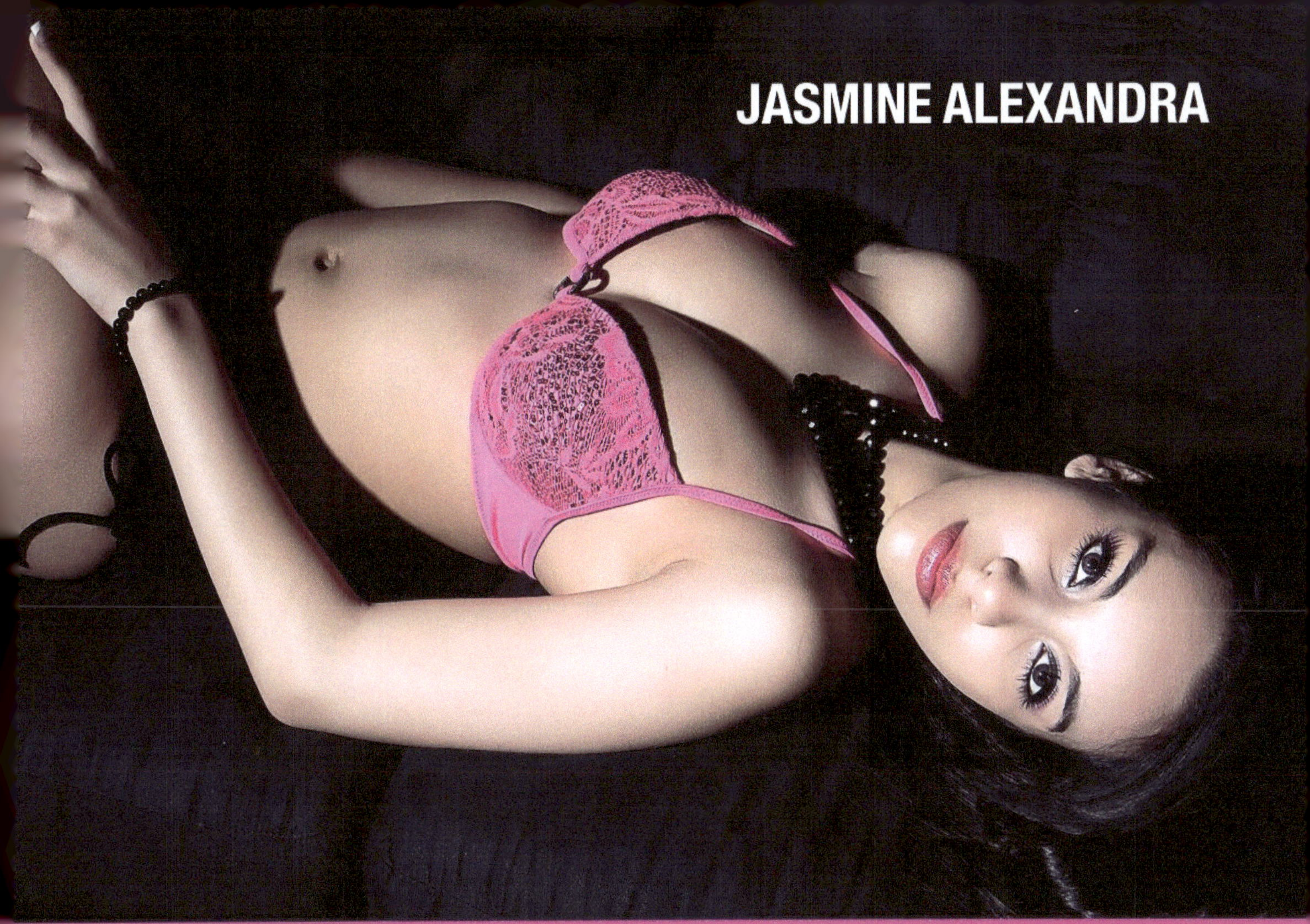

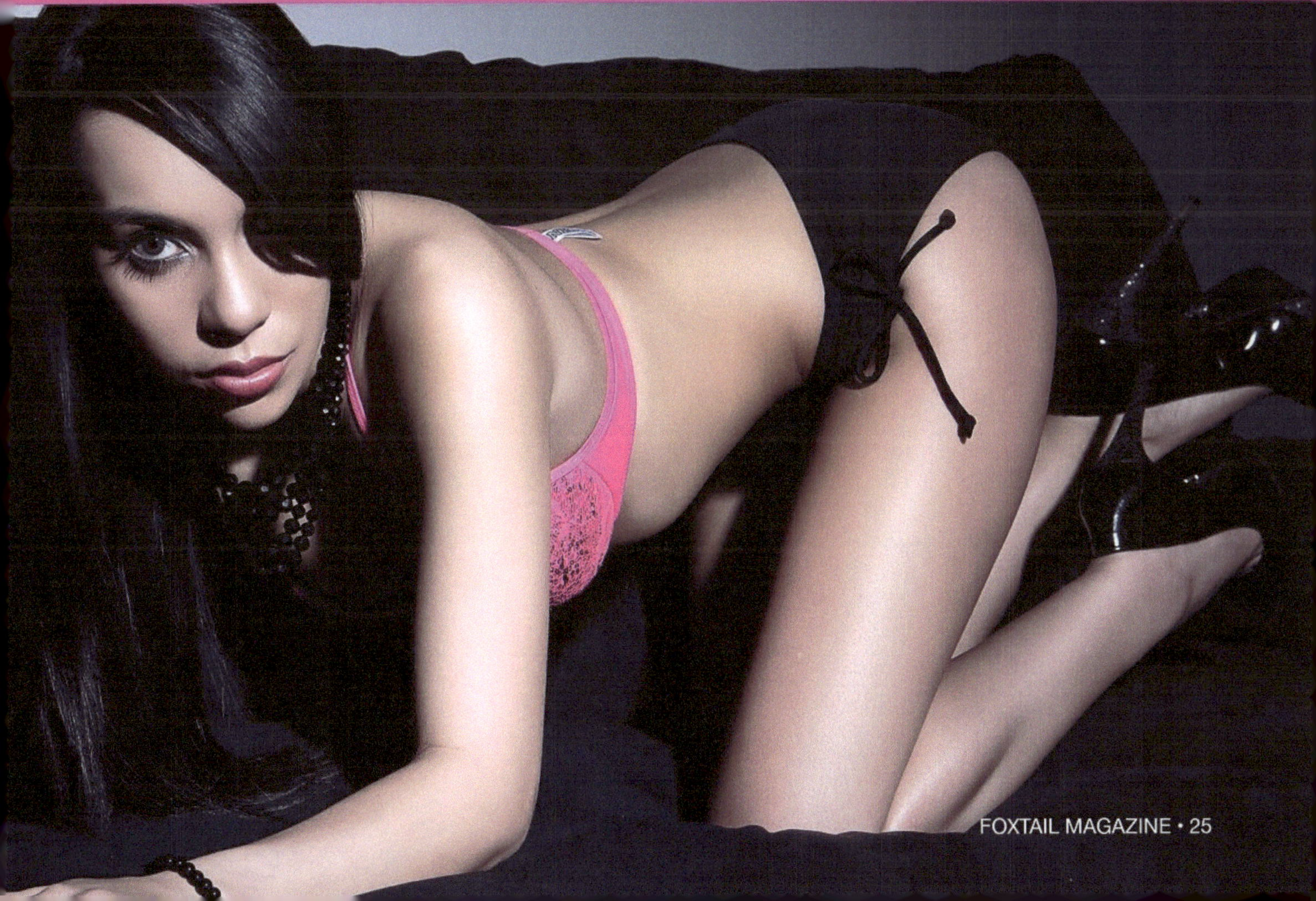

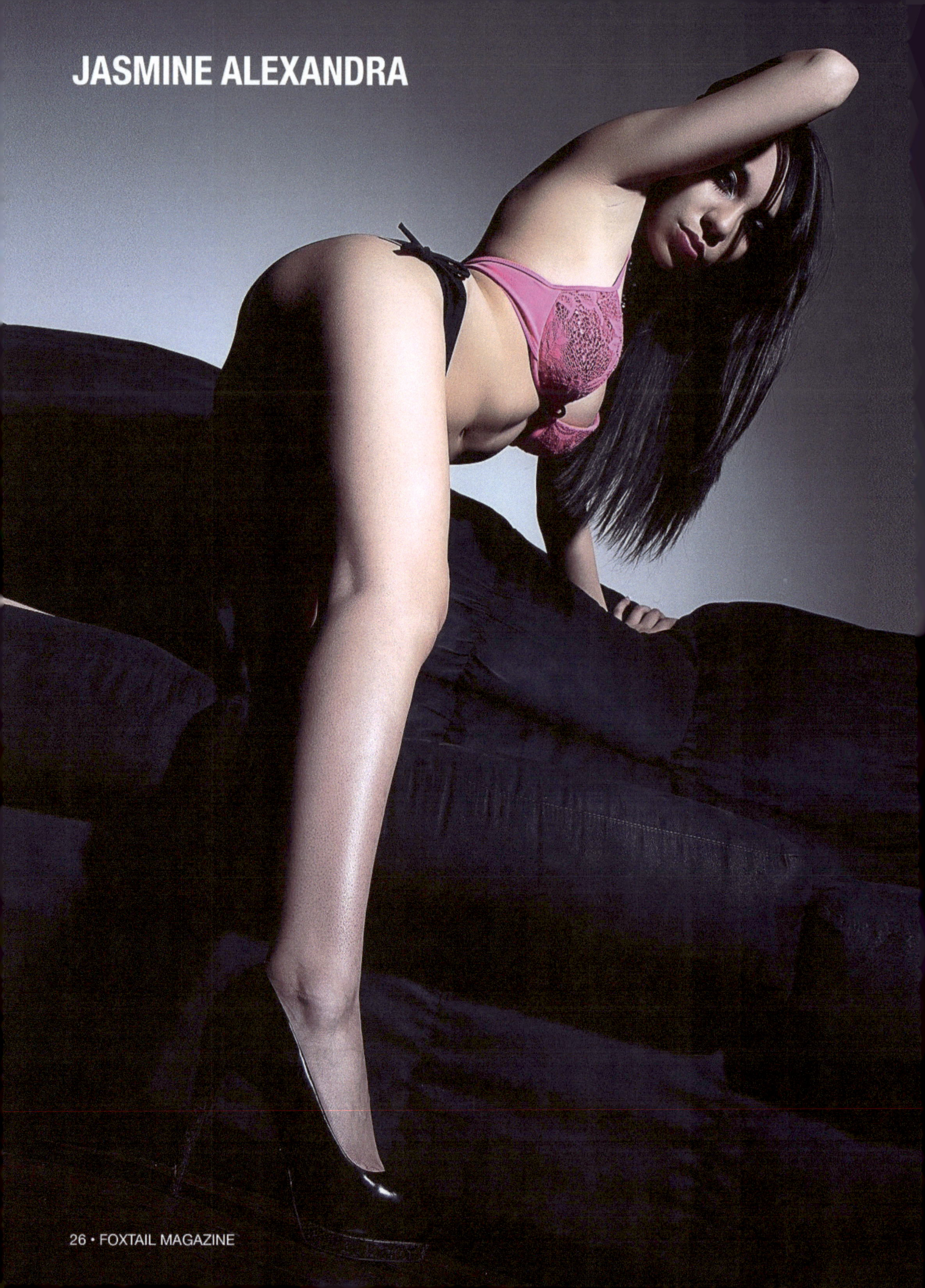

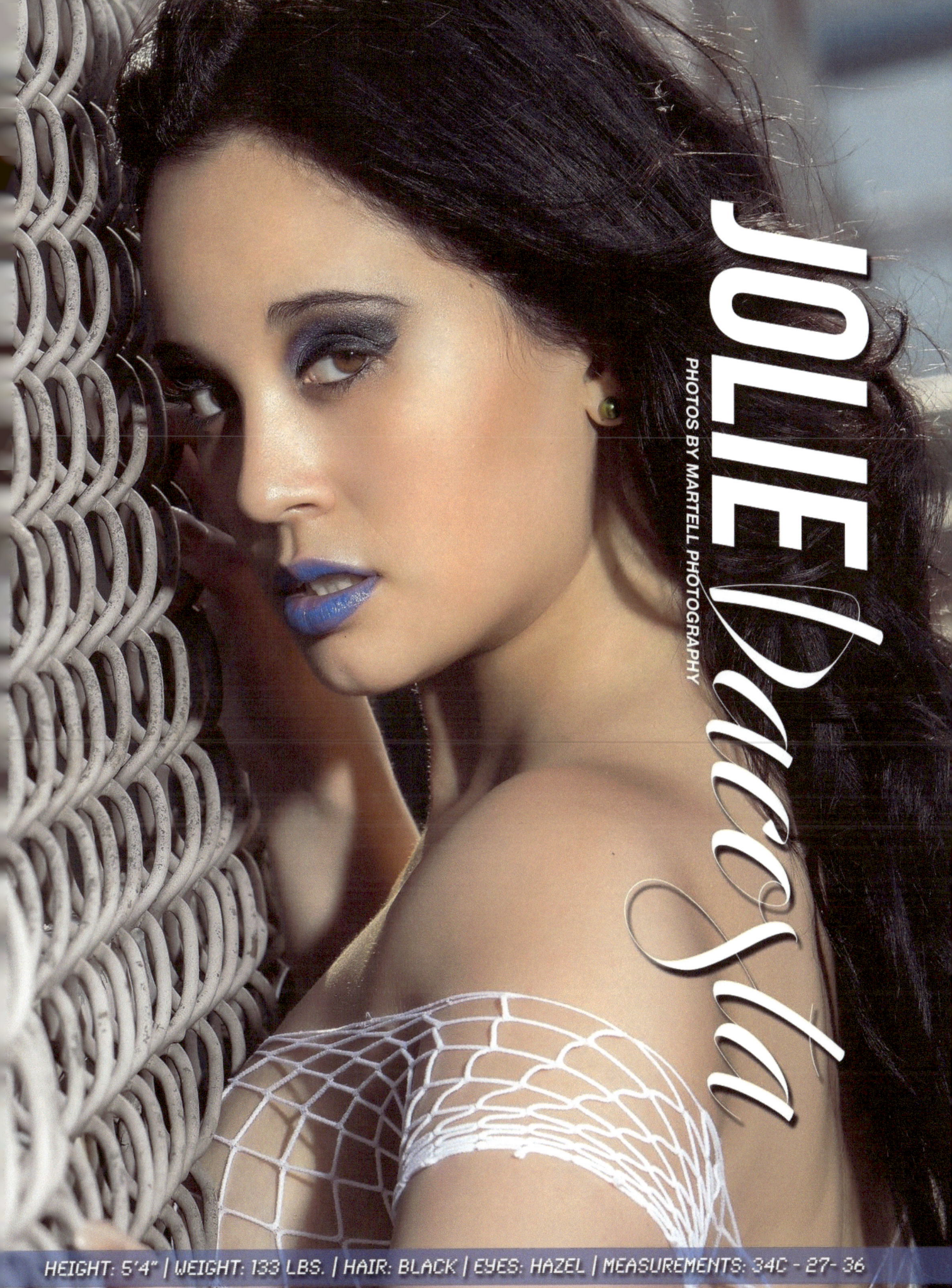

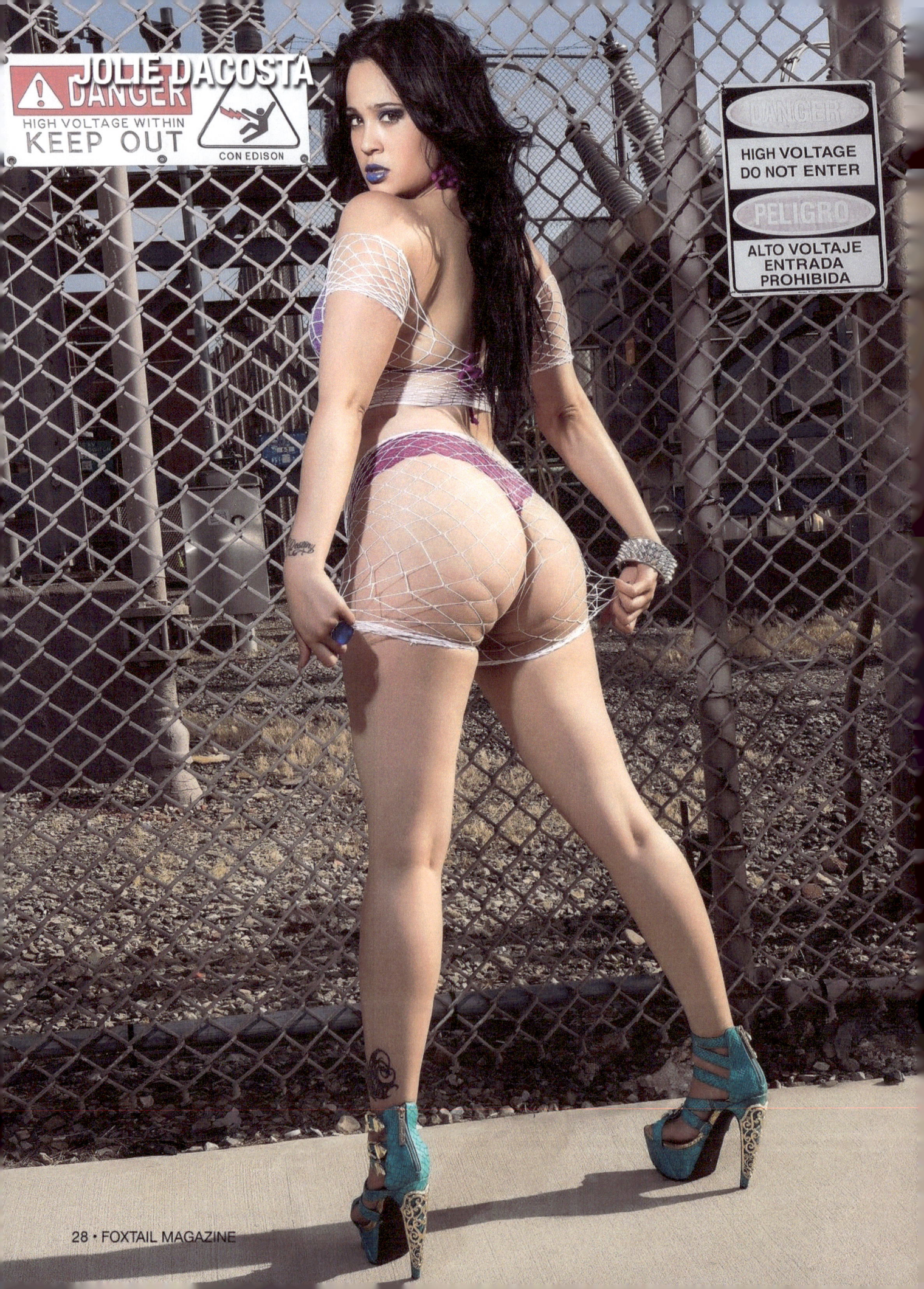

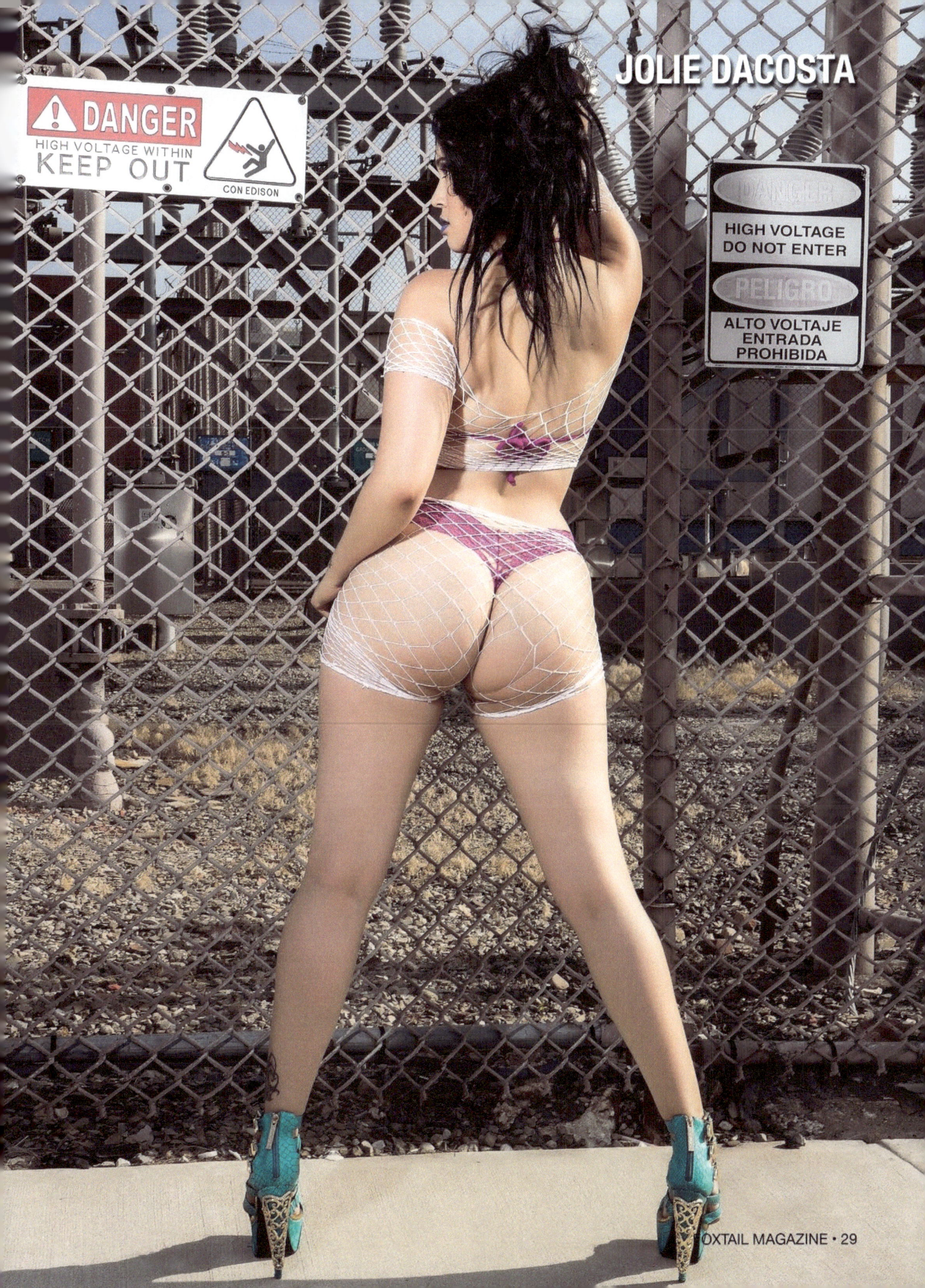

JOLIE DACOSTA

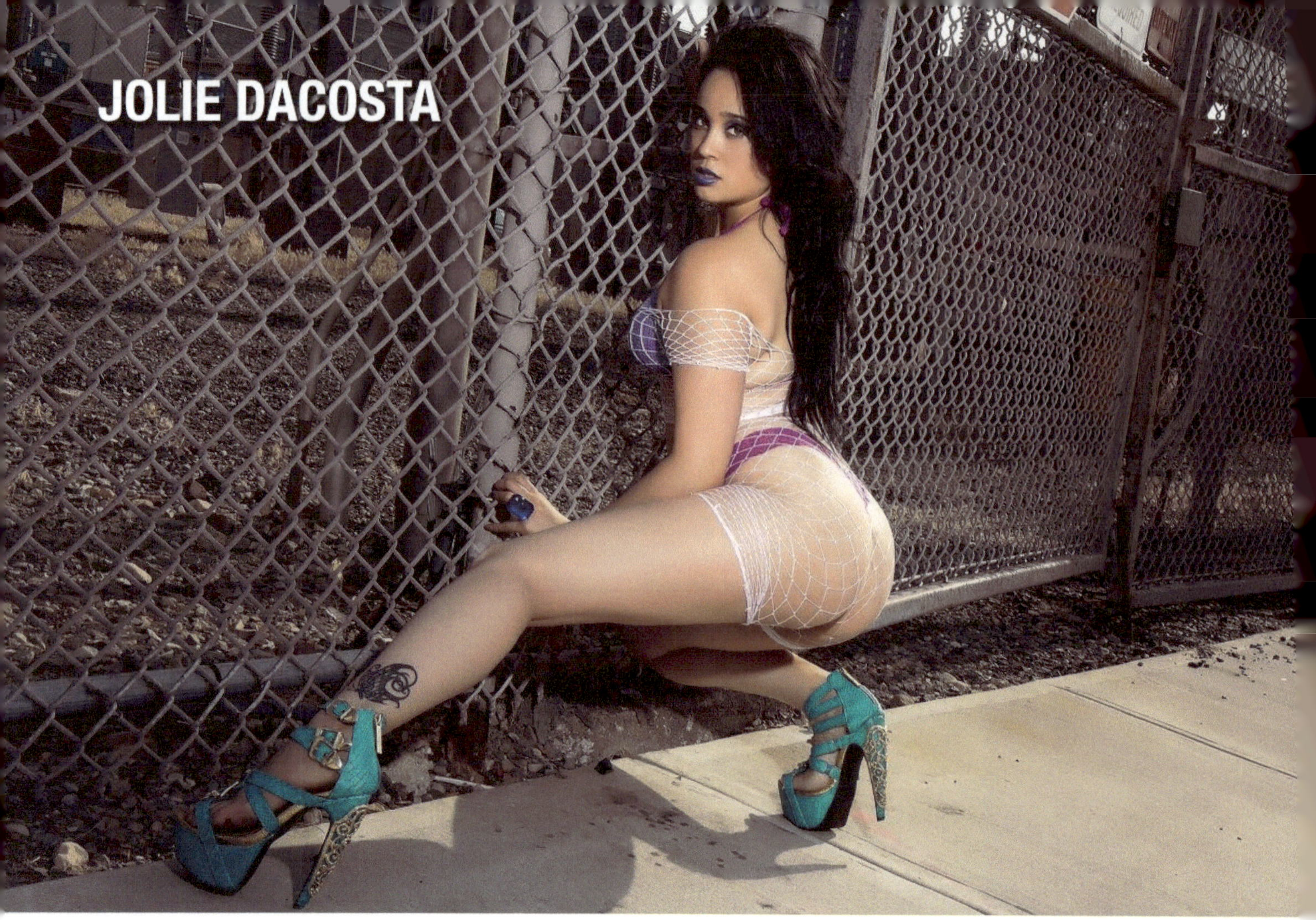

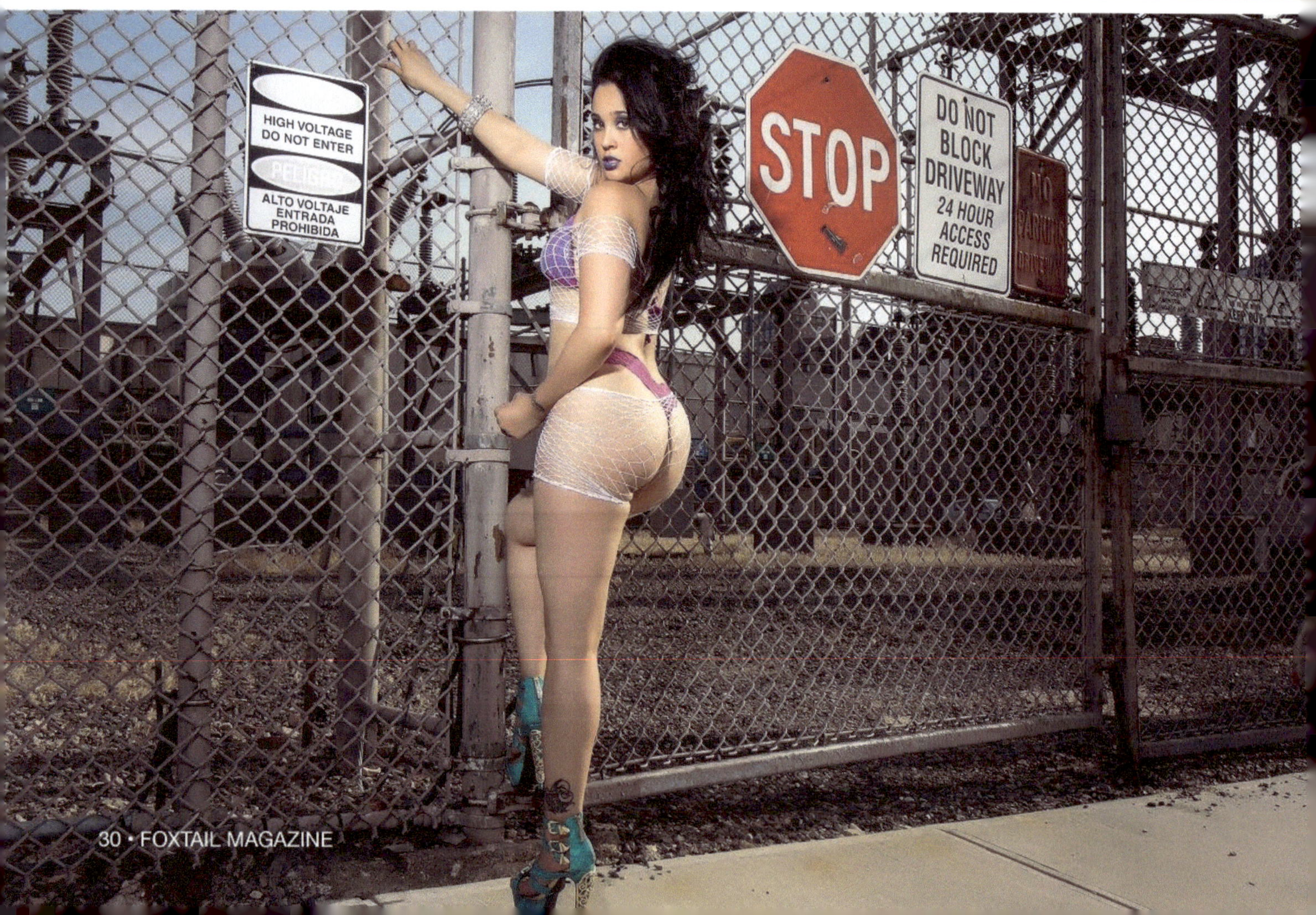

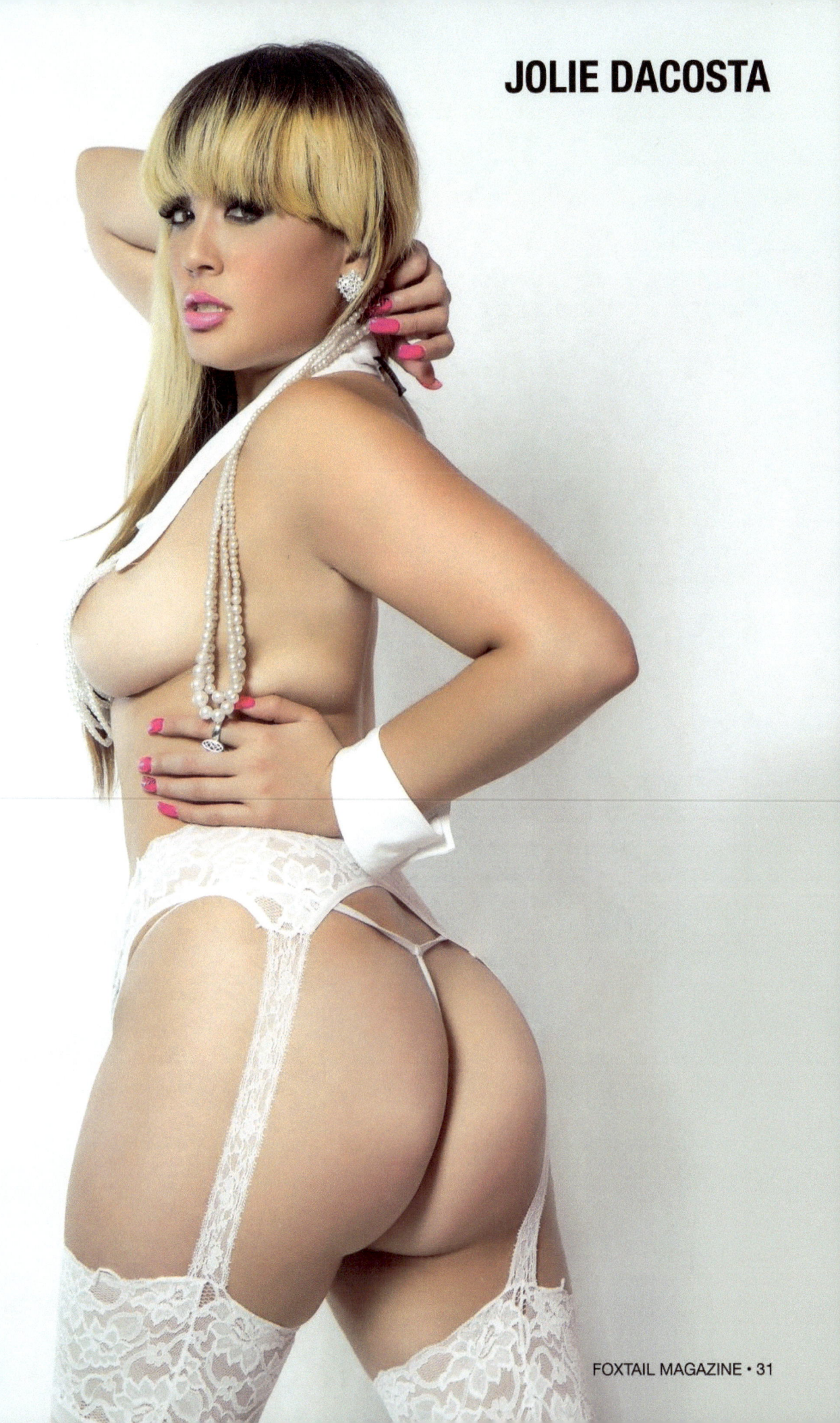

JOLIE DACOSTA

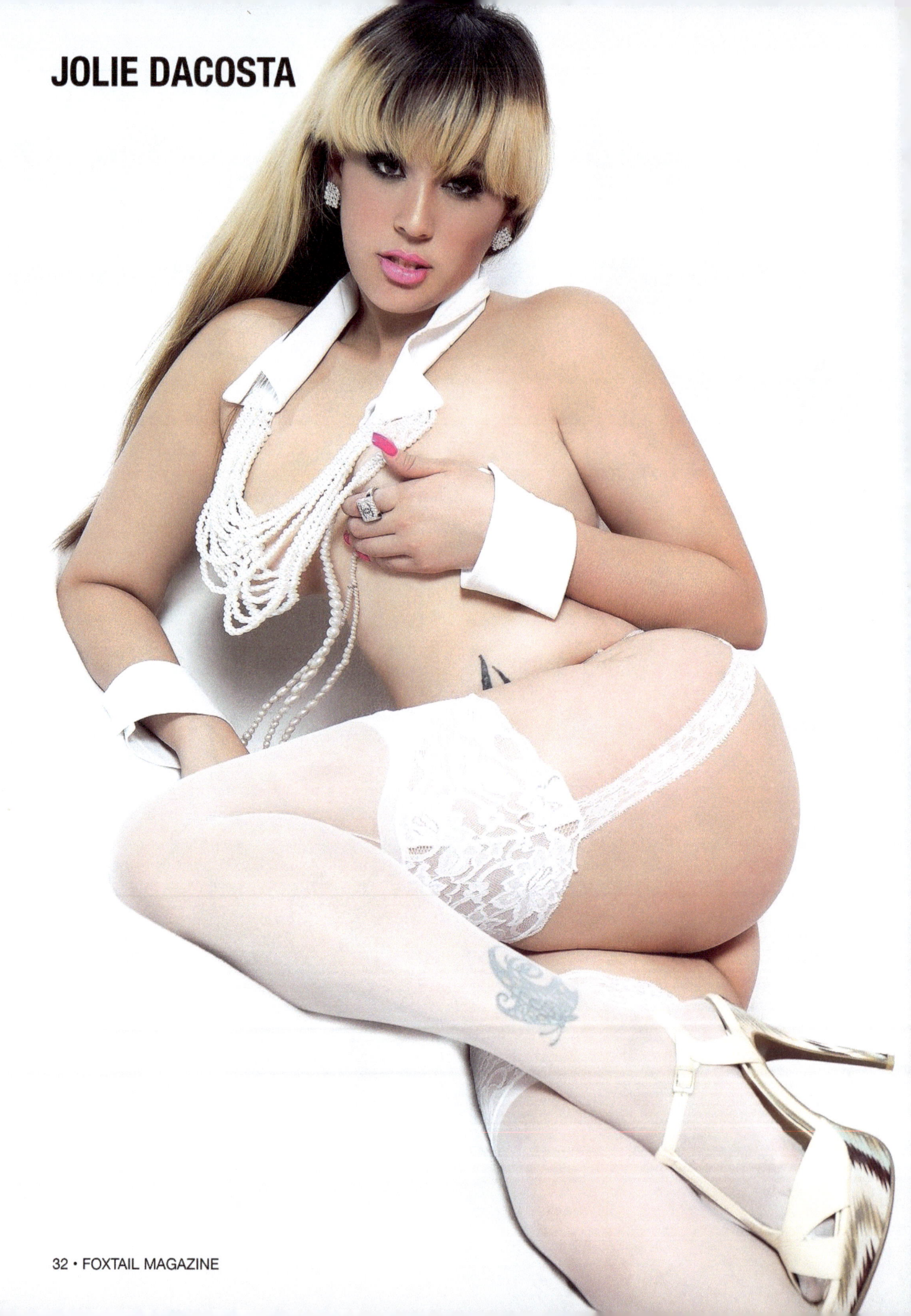

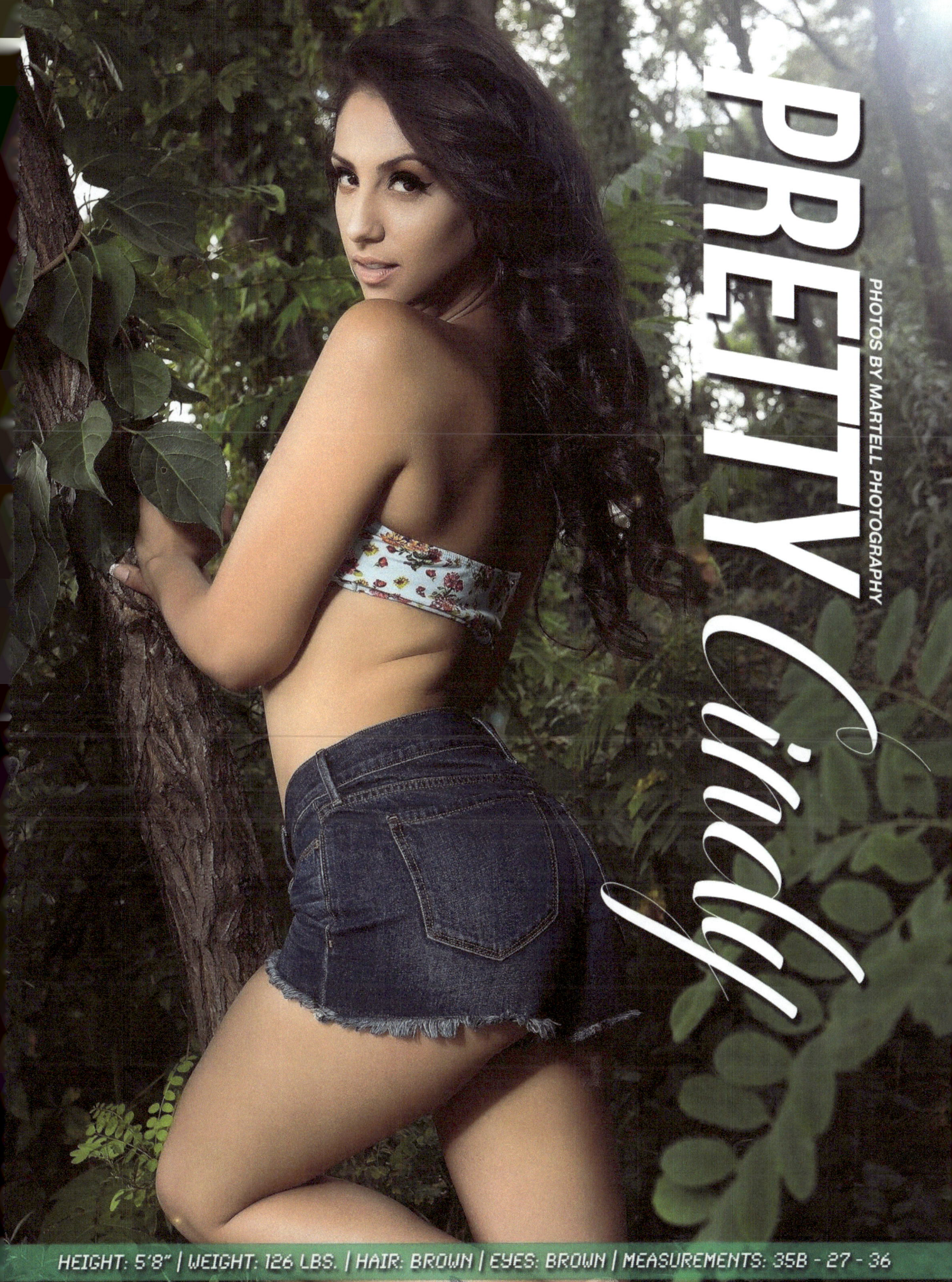

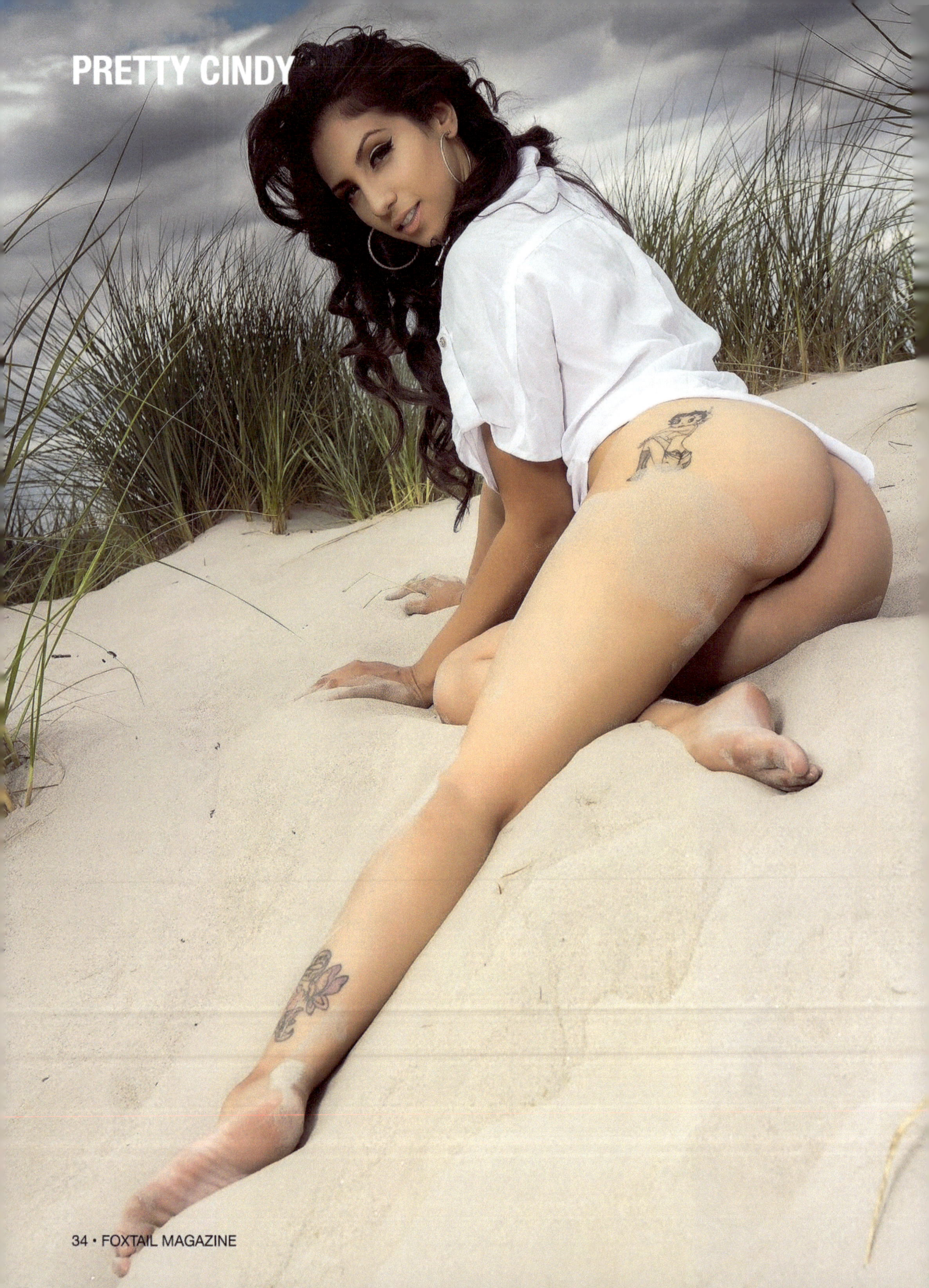

PRETTY CINDY

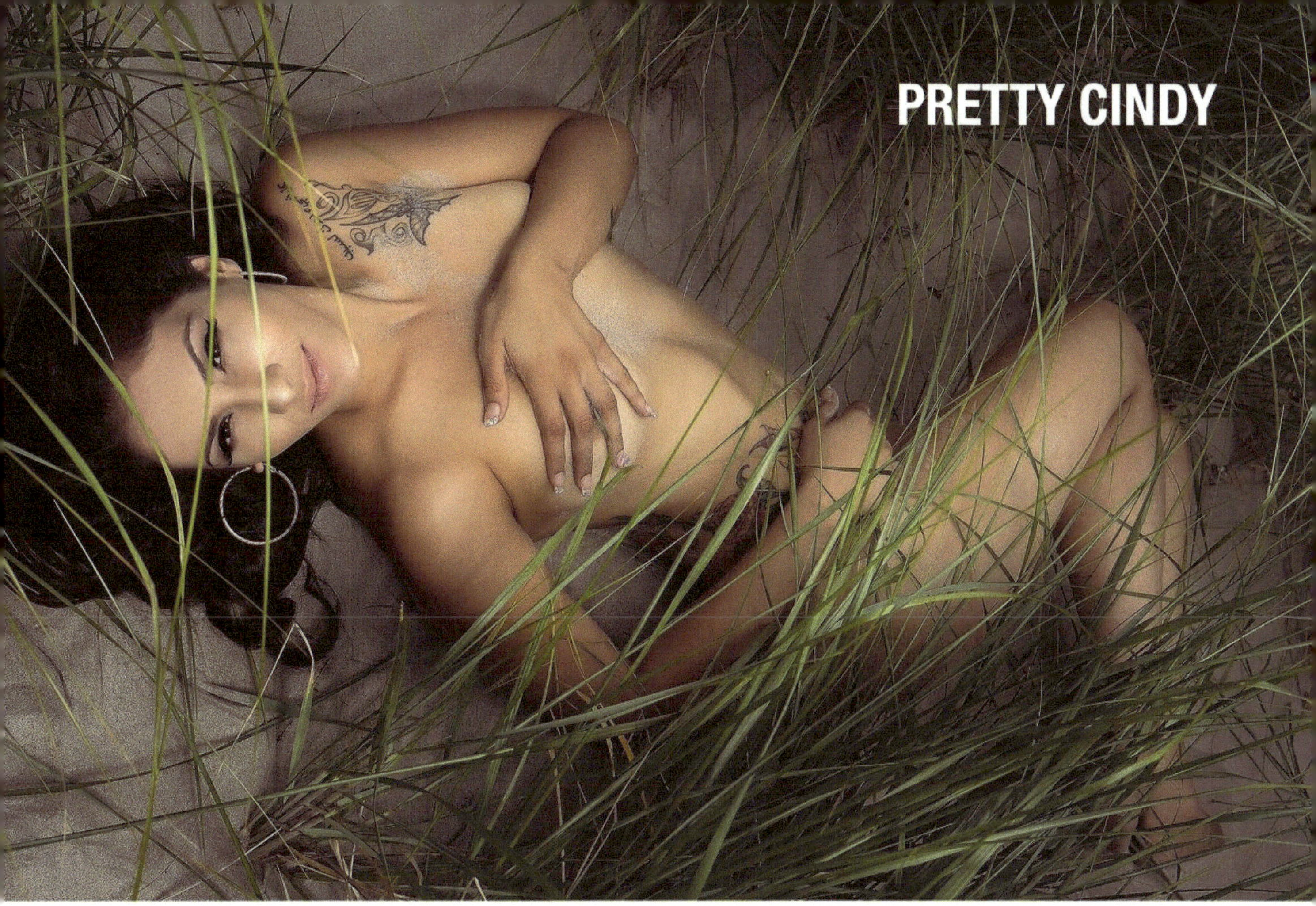

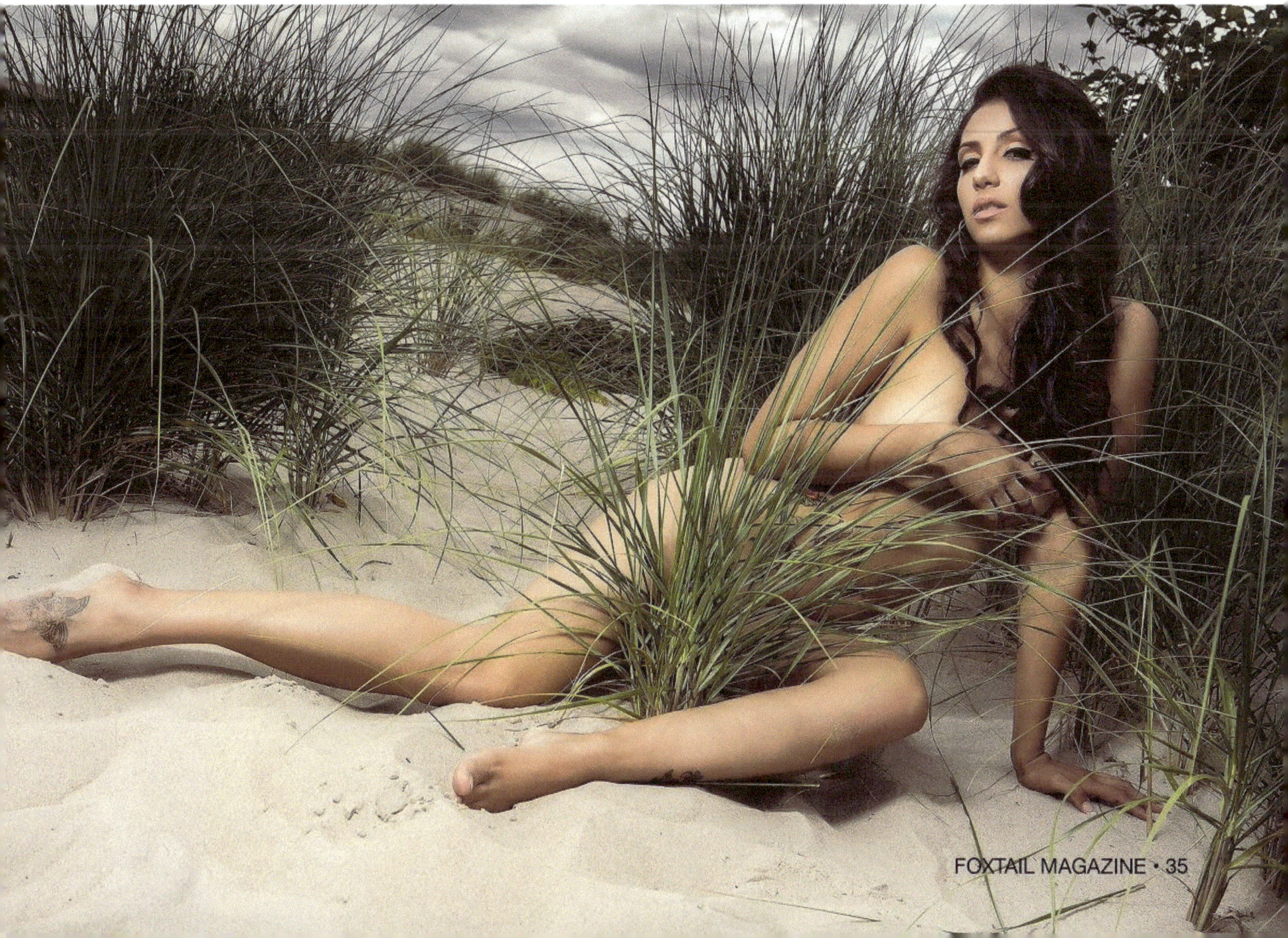

PRETTY CINDY

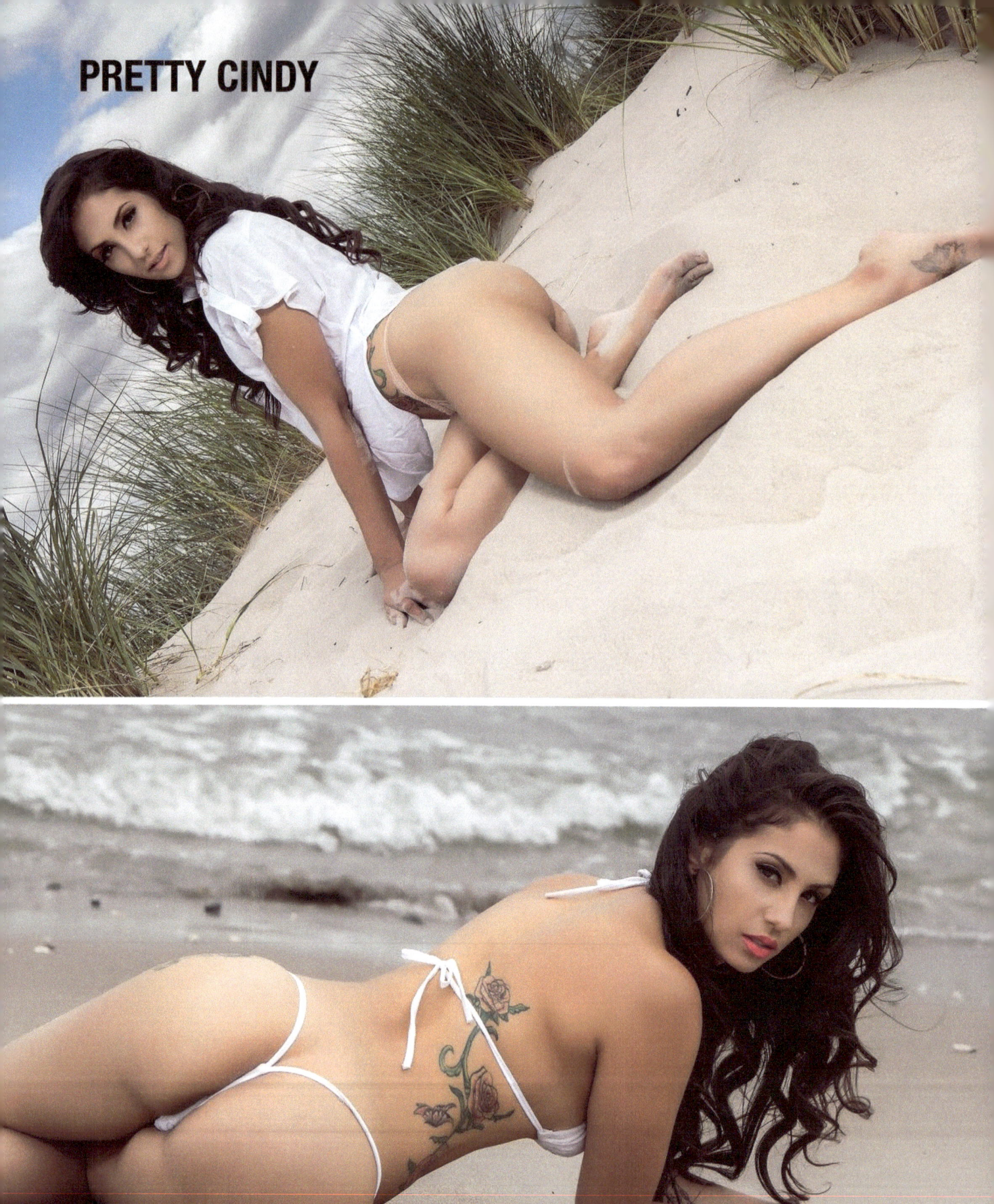

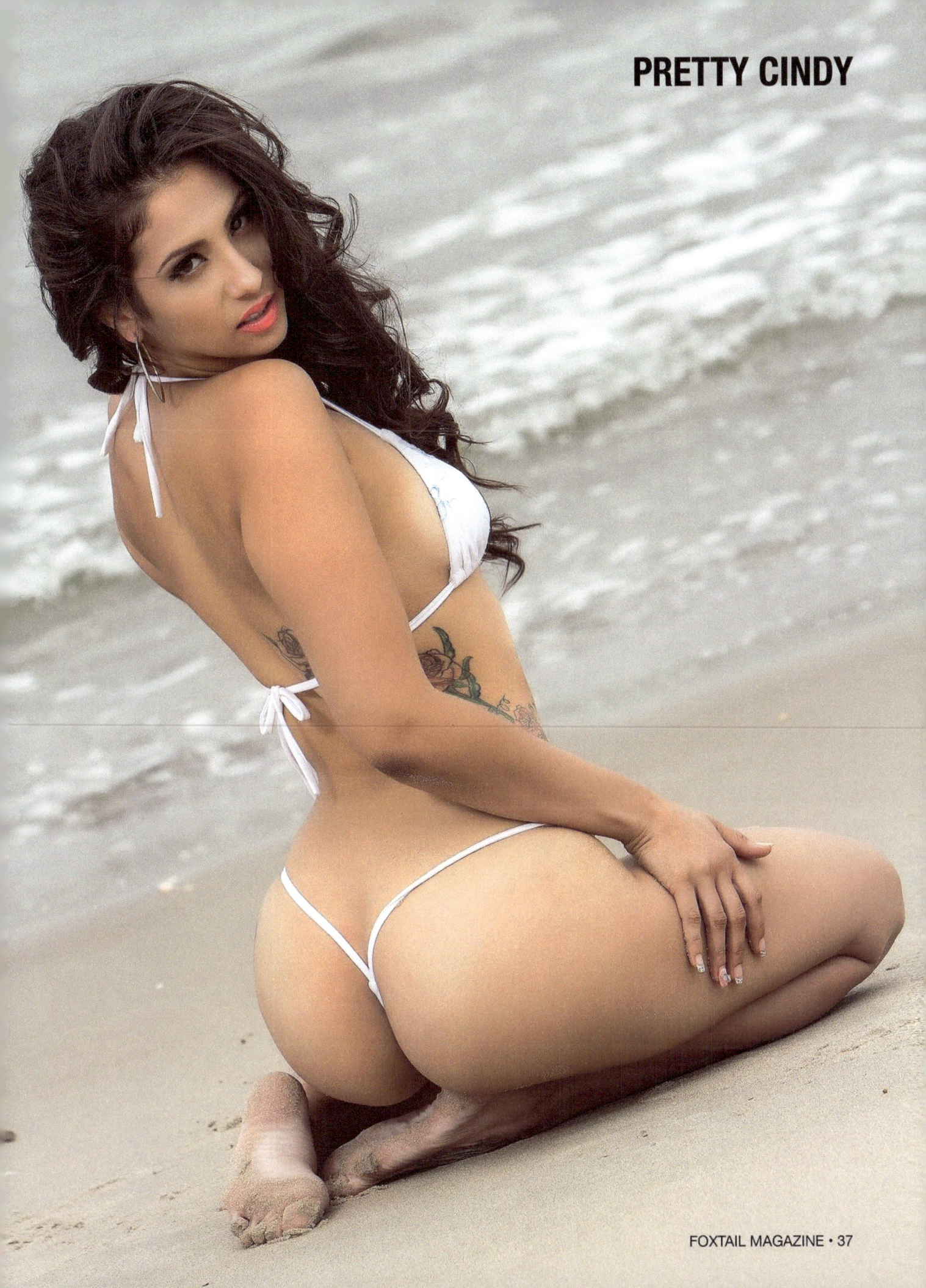

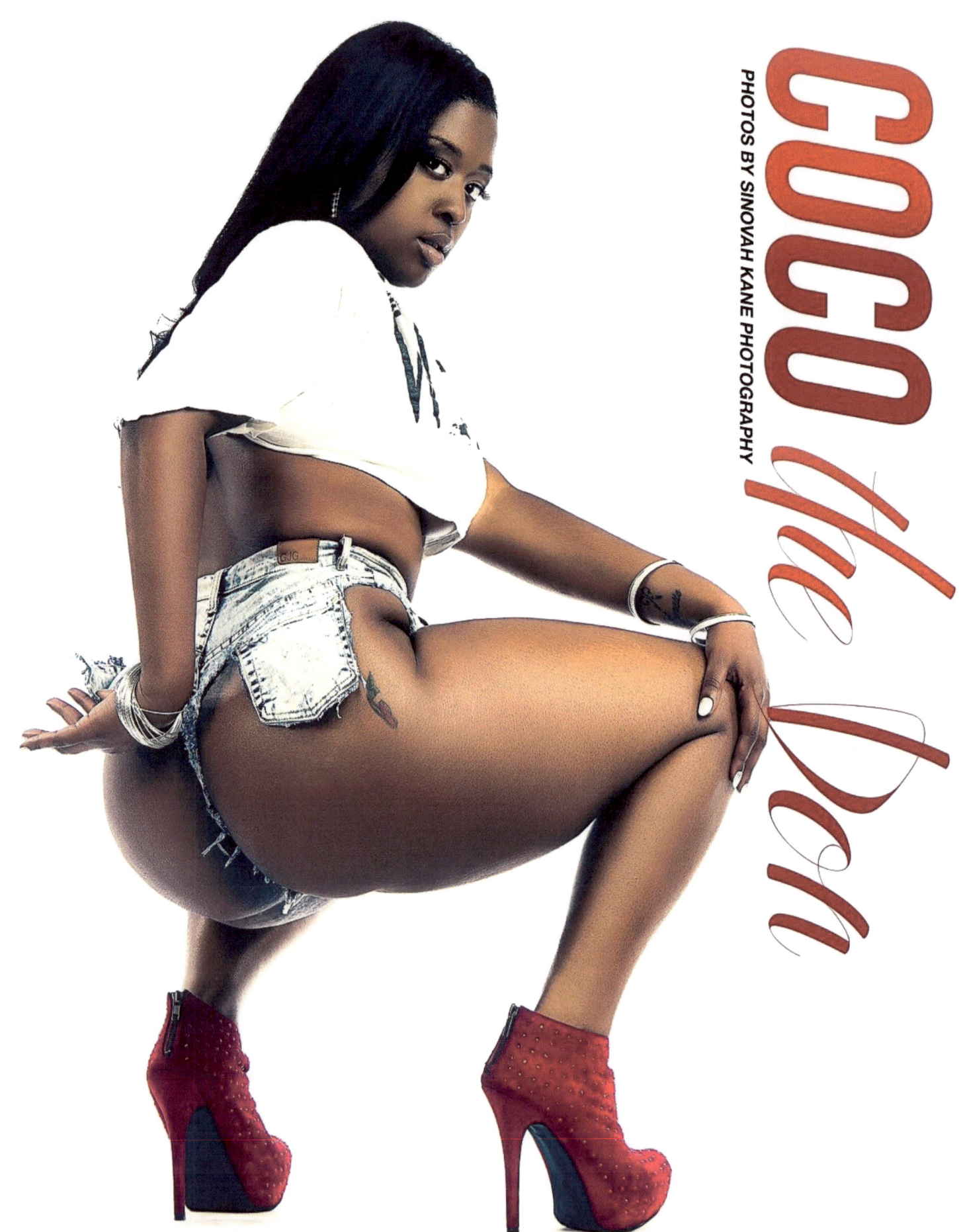

COCO the Don

PHOTOS BY SINOVAH KANE PHOTOGRAPHY

HEIGHT: 5'5" | WEIGHT: 150 LBS. | HAIR: BLACK | EYES: BROWN | MEASUREMENTS: 38DD-28-42

COCO THA DON

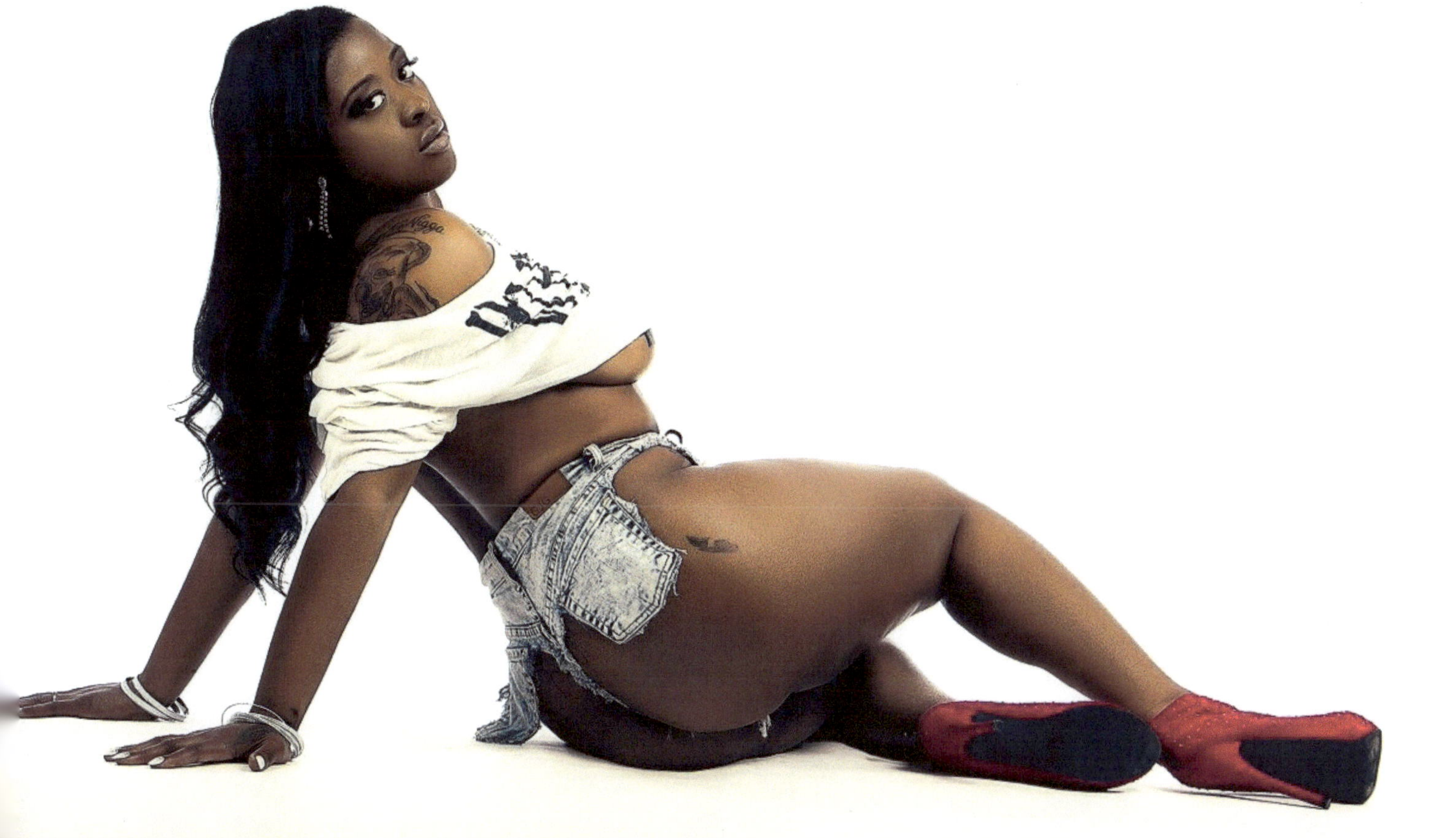

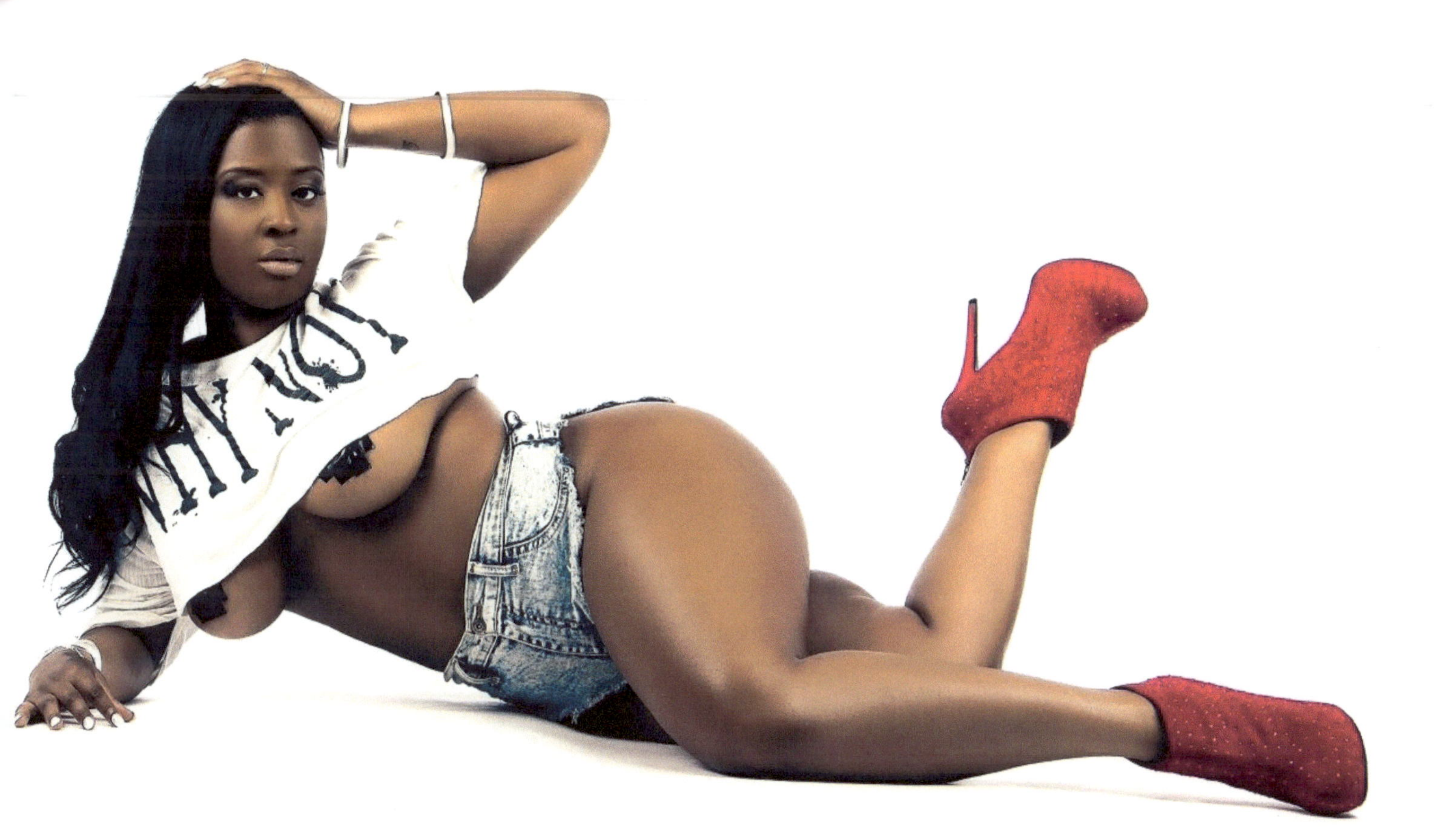

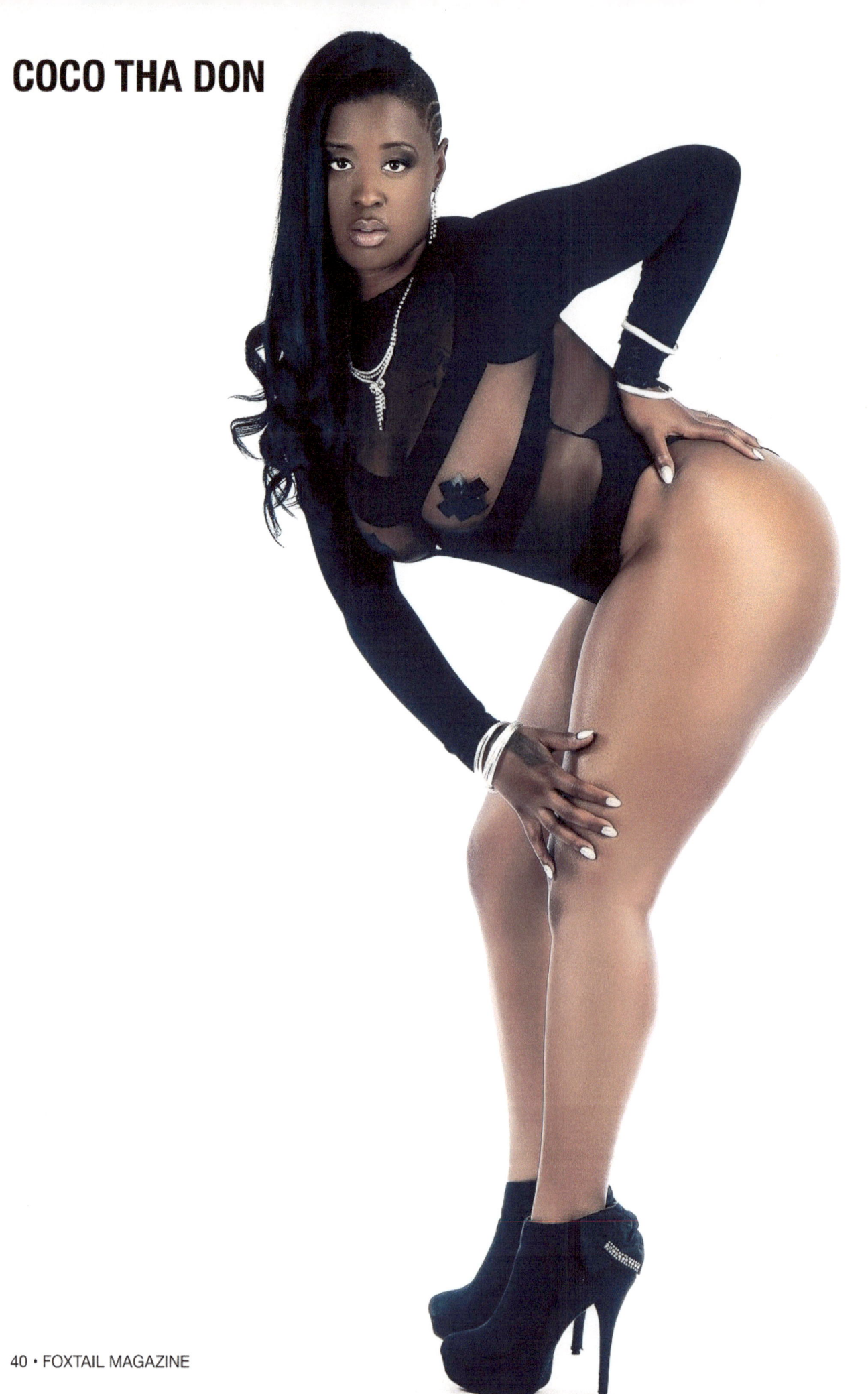

COCO THA DON

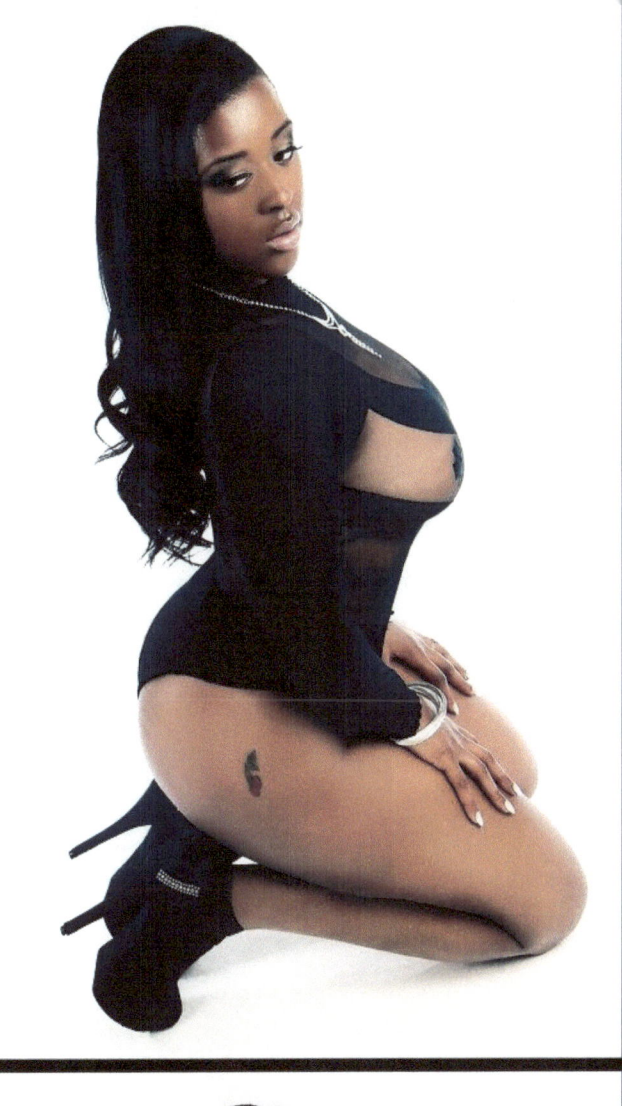
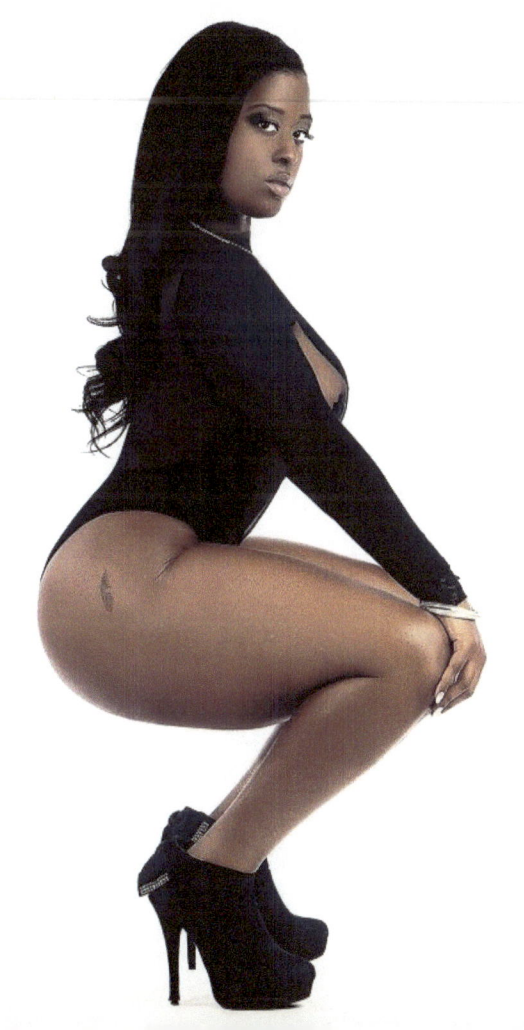

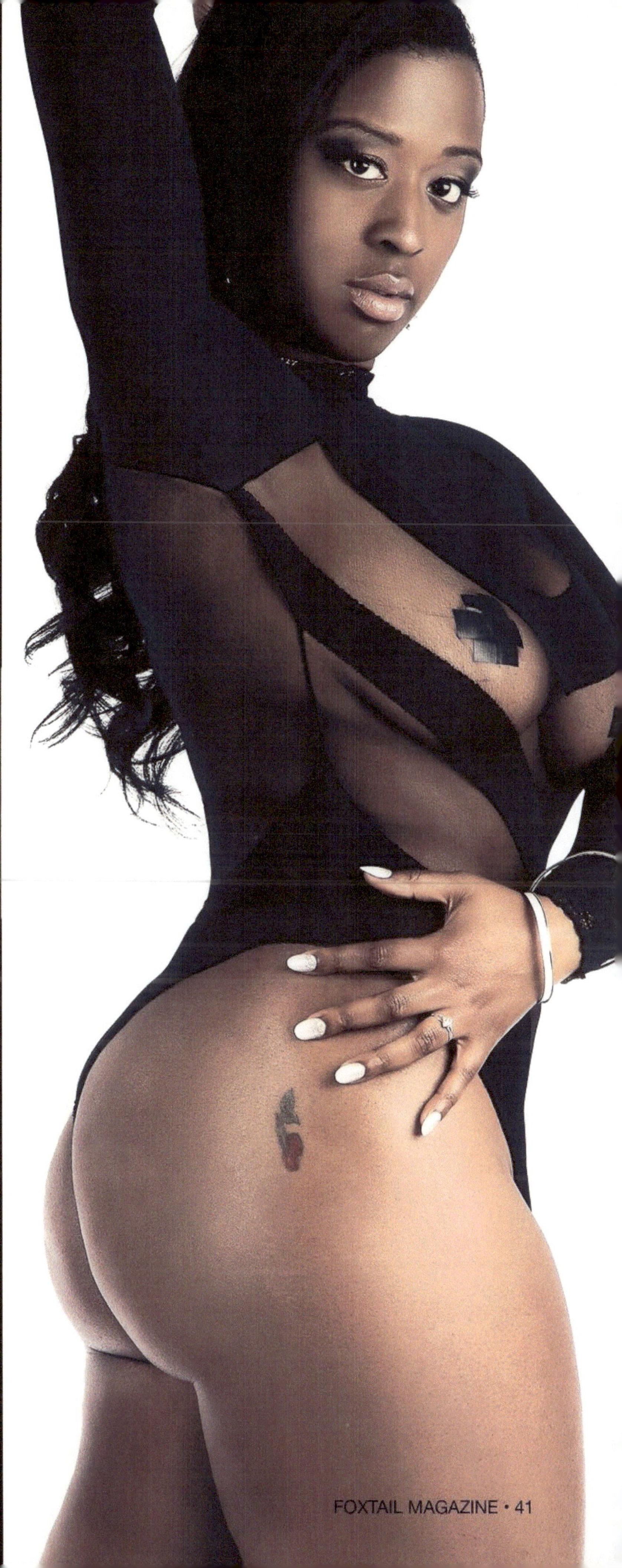

FOXTAIL MAGAZINE • 41

FOXTAIL MAGAZINE

Next UP . . .

China Girl

PUT DOWN YOUR

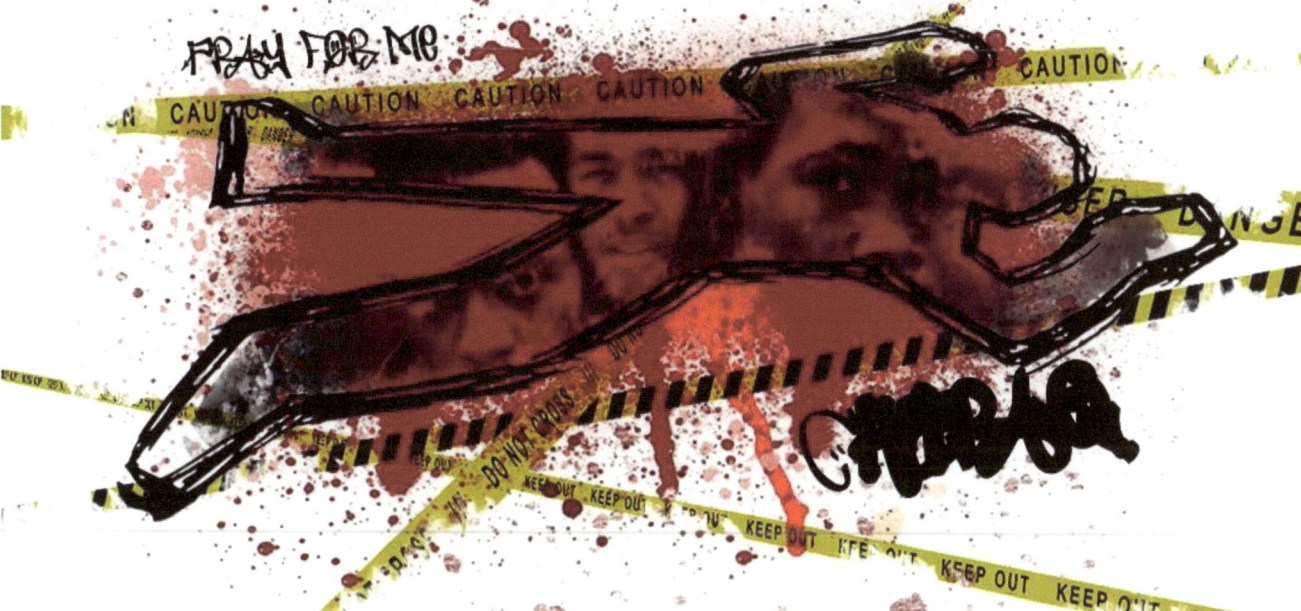

GUNS CHICAGO

FOXTAIL MAGAZINE

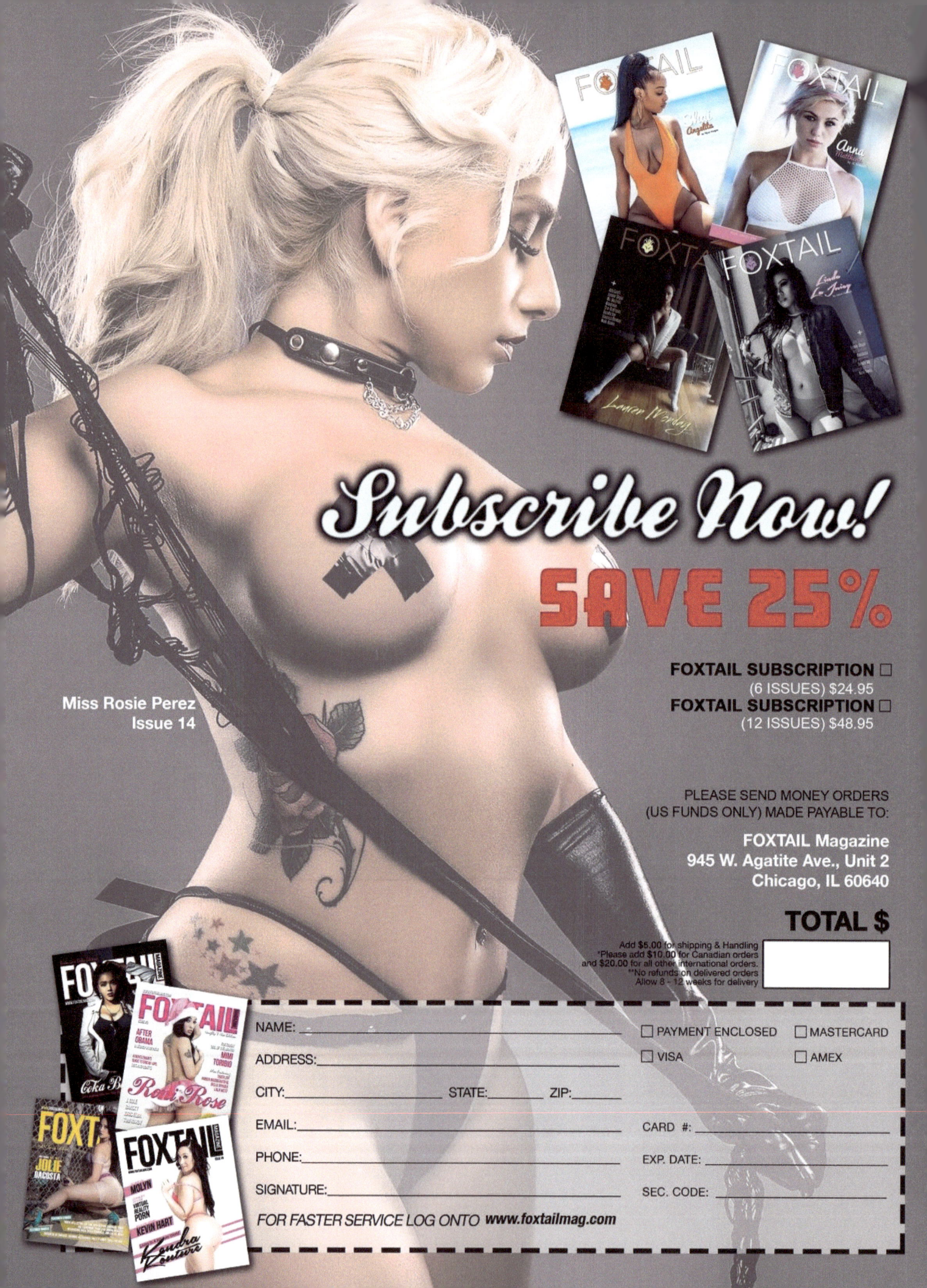

GET **FOXTAIL** MAGAZINE
On the Devices that Matter to You the Most!!!

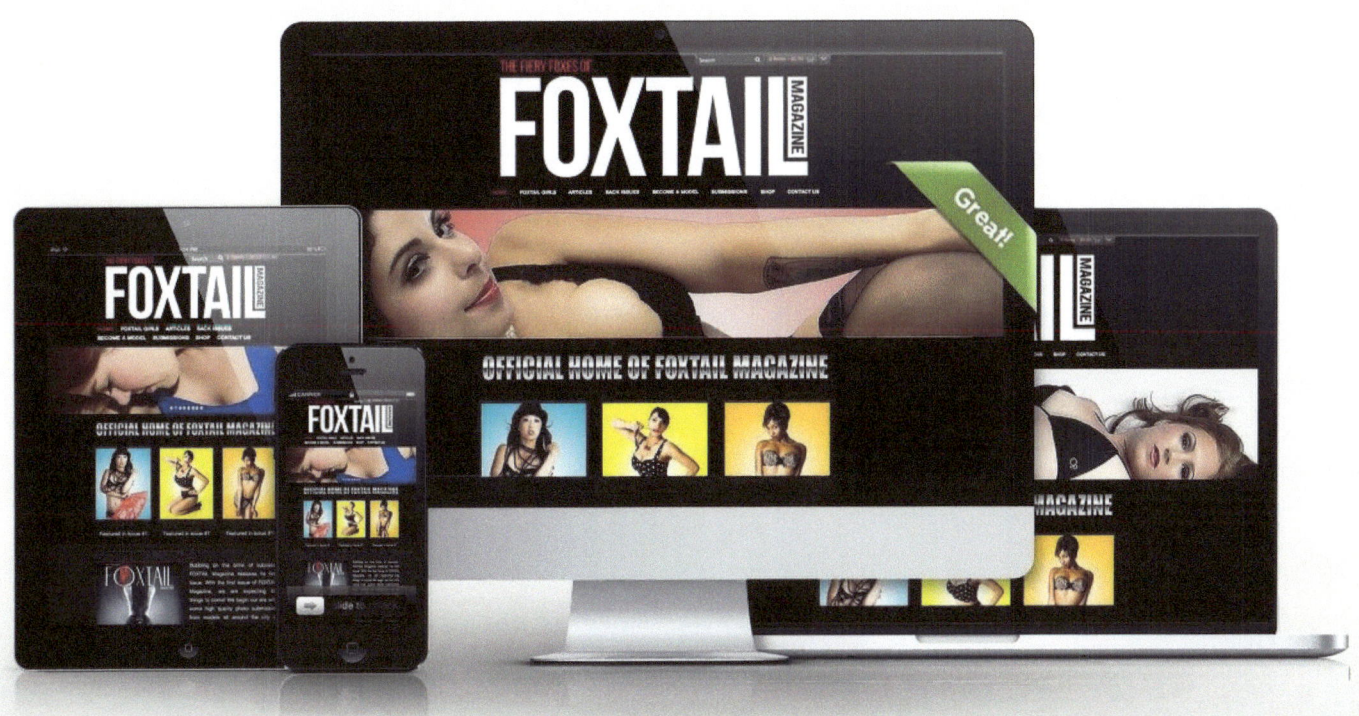

ADVERTISE
WITH
FOXTAIL MAGAZINE

FOR MORE INFOMATION, SEND EMAIL TO: ADVERTISING@FOXTAILMAG.COM

www.ingramcontent.com/pod-product-compliance
Lightning Source LLC
Chambersburg PA
CBHW040409220526
45473CB00004B/1179